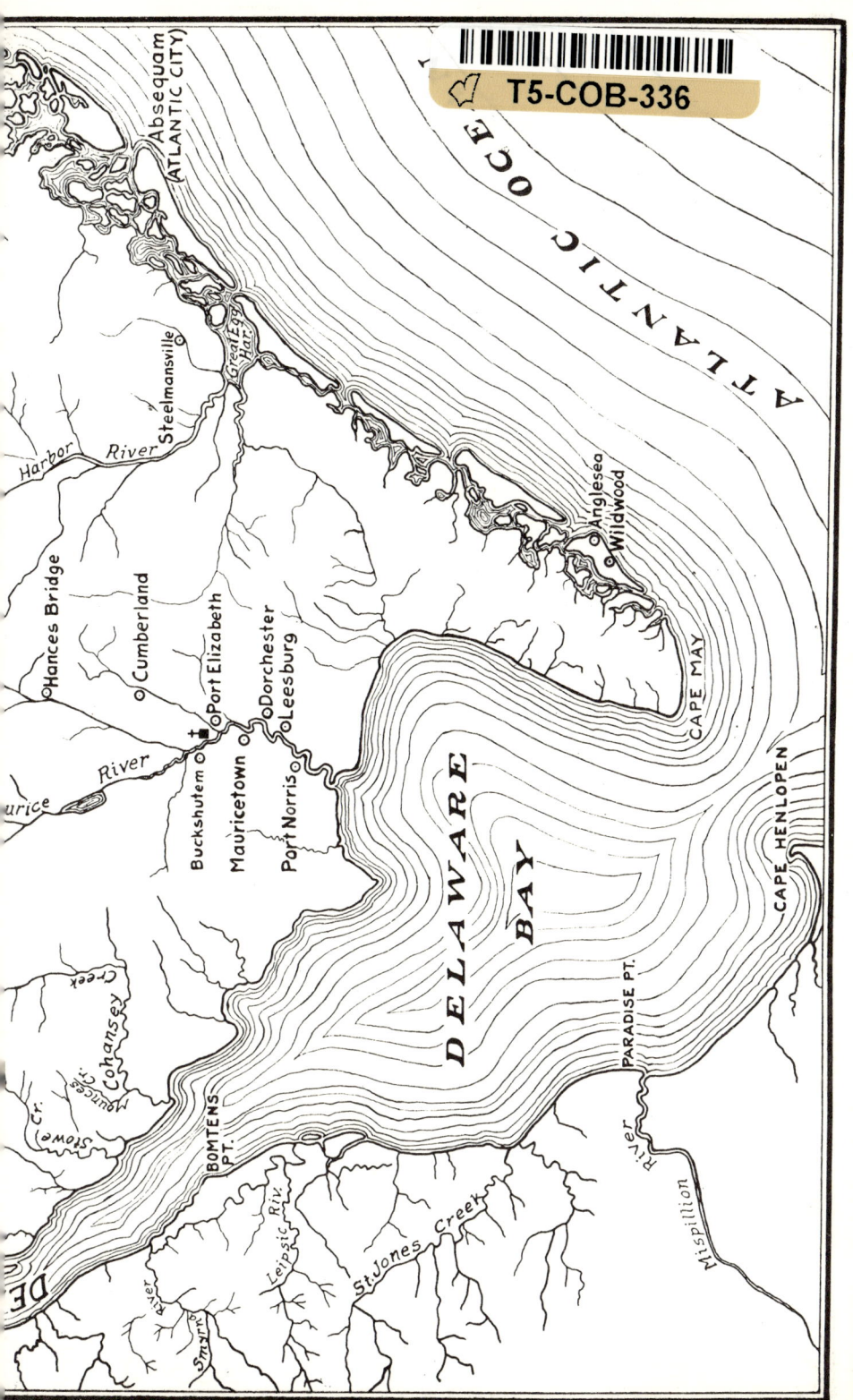

FEDERAL WRITERS' PROJECT
AMERICAN GUIDE SERIES

THE
SWEDES and FINNS
IN NEW JERSEY

AMS PRESS

NEW YORK

Trinity Church Steeple, Swedesboro

THE
SWEDES and FINNS
IN NEW JERSEY

AMERICAN GUIDE SERIES

Written and Illustrated by the
Federal Writers' Project of the
Works Progress Administration
State of New Jersey

With an Introduction by
Dr. Amandus Johnson
Director of the American Swedish Historical Museum,
Philadelphia, Pa.

Sponsored by
The New Jersey Commission to Commemorate the 300th Anniversary
of the Settlement by the Swedes and Finns on the Delaware

D. STEWART CRAVEN, *Chairman*

1938

Library of Congress Cataloging in Publication Data

Federal Writers' Project. New Jersey.
   The Swedes and Finns in New Jersey.

   At head of half-title: Federal Writers' Project.
   Original ed. issued in the American guide series.
   "Sponsored by the New Jersey Commission to Commemorate the 300th Anniversary of the Settlement by the Swedes and Finns on the Delaware."
   Bibliography: p.
   1. New Jersey—History—Colonial period.   2. New Sweden—History.   3. Swedes in New Jersey.   4. Finns in New Jersey. I. Federal Writers' Project.   II. Title.   III. Series: American guide series.
F137.F32   1975   917.49'06'397   73-3640
ISBN 0-404-57940-X

Reprinted from the edition of 1938, Bayonne
First AMS edition published in 1975
Manufactured in the United States of America

AMS PRESS INC.
NEW YORK, N.Y. 10003

Works Progress Administration

Harry L. Hopkins, *Administrator*
Ellen S. Woodward, *Assistant Administrator*
Henry G. Alsberg, *Director of Federal Writers' Project*

The New Jersey Commission to Commemorate the 300th Anniversary of the Settlement by the Swedes and Finns on the Delaware

Senators: D. Stewart Craven, Salem, *Chairman*; Albert E. Burling, Camden; Robert C. Hendrickson, Woodbury; George H. Stanger, Vineland.

Assemblymen: Millard E. Allen, Laurel Springs; Lawrence H. Ellis, Haddonfield; Norman P. Featherer, Penns Grove; Howard B. Hancock, Greenwich; Rocco Palese, Camden; John G. Sholl, Pitman.

Commissioners: Frank I. Liveright, Newark, *Vice Chairman, North Jersey*; Loyal D. Odhner, Camden, *Vice Chairman, South Jersey*; Harry C. Hallberg, Orange; George de B. Keim, Edgewater Park; Karl J. Olson, East Orange; Samuel H. Richards, Collingswood.

Secretary: Ann G. Craven, Salem.

PREFACE

THE FEDERAL WRITERS' PROJECT OF NEW JERSEY *has prepared this volume as part of the Nation-wide celebration of the three hundredth anniversary of the landing of the Swedes and Finns on American soil. In addition to its program of guidebooks for the forty-eight States, the Federal Writers' Project is recording the development of various racial and national groups which have made a contribution to American culture.*

This book is one step in the New Jersey Project's aim to recreate the history of the State in terms of the peoples who have shared in its growth. The Swedes and Finns *serves two purposes: it describes the settlement and development of a section of the Delaware River Valley, and pictures the process of Swedish and Finnish assimilation in New Jersey. It is one State's record of the activities of important groups which spread over the entire Nation.*

The Federal Writers' Project of New Jersey has welcomed the opportunity of cooperating with the New Jersey Commission established to celebrate this anniversary of national and international importance. The project is grateful to many persons and institutions for assistance and advice in the preparation of this volume. We are especially indebted to Dr. Amandus Johnson, director of the American Swedish Historical Museum, and to Dr. John H. Wuorinen of Columbia University, who read and criticized the entire manuscript and offered many valuable suggestions.

For cooperation on chapters dealing with their special interests, we are grateful to Frank H. Stewart, president of the Gloucester County Historical Society; Professor A. M.

SWEDES AND FINNS

Carlson, Upsala College; and the Rev. T. A. Gustafson, pastor of Lebanon Lutheran Church, West New York, N. J.

We also wish to acknowledge the assistance of the Camden County Library, the American Swedish Historical Museum, the Free Public Library of Newark, the Historical Society of Pennsylvania, the Free Library of Philadelphia, the Gloucester County Historical Society, the Salem County Historical Society, the Camden County Historical Society, and the Episcopal Churches of Swedesboro and Churchtown, which permitted the translation of their Swedish records.

IRENE FUHLBRUEGGE
State Director

INTRODUCTION

I HAVE read the manuscript of this little book with much pleasure. I have found little to alter and less to correct. In a manner it is a pioneer work—the first time that a single volume has been devoted to the Swedish settlements in New Jersey. The material for the early history of western New Jersey is meager. With the exception of some references and paragraphs in English, Swedish and Dutch records about the English and Swedish settlements at present Salem (Fort New Elfsborg) and the Dutch settlements at Fort Nassau, and about Swedish, English and Dutch land purchases, there is practically nothing to throw light on the history of the eastern shore of the Delaware until well on towards the last quarter of the 17th century.

When the English took over the Delaware region in 1664, the settlements on the New Jersey side were so little known or considered so unimportant that they are not even mentioned in the articles of surrender, or in other papers drawn up at the time about the district. We are certain that many Swedes and Finns several years before had crossed the river and erected their log cabins and broken ground for fields and orchards; but neither letters to friends and relations in the old country nor other sources about them have come down to us. The only references to their activities are found in deeds and land purchases of a later period and from these we must construct our story as best we can.

The religious life of the settlers has fared better, as the church records, reports and letters to the mother country give a fairly complete picture of this part of their history.

SWEDES AND FINNS

This history, however, begins in 1701—beyond that all is darkness, except for some gleams of light that we can bring to bear by reconstruction or assumption. The main source of this religious history of the Swedes in New Jersey (which also throws light on the extent of their settlements, their manner of life, etc.) is the church records of Raccoon (Swedesboro) and Penns Neck, and the journals and letters of the Swedish pastors of this district, preserved in the archives of Uppsala, Sweden. With the exception of the use I have made of these sources in my articles and books, this is the first time that the manuscripts in these two churches have been extensively employed, mainly because the early ones are in Swedish, and hence available to but few. This volume, therefore, brings out a number of facts not printed before.

The volume is a welcome contribution to the history of the Swedes and Finns in New Jersey and the authors are to be congratulated on their achievement. The volume should not only arouse an interest in the history of the early Swedes in New Jersey. It should teach a lesson and be an inspiration to us by its narratives of hardships and struggles and sacrifices. These early pioneers conquered a wilderness and laid the foundation upon which their descendants built and we build further. Times have changed since these early days. We often complain of hardships, we often think we suffer want, but even the poorest among us lives in luxury compared to the lot of these early settlers. The average citizen of Swedesboro today has more comforts than a king or mighty potentate enjoyed 300 years ago. These early settlers in western New Jersey would walk many miles and finally cross a great river to attend church at Tinicum Island or at Wicacoa. Even after the church was built at Raccoon (Swedes-

INTRODUCTION

boro) many a settler with his family would have to walk from five to ten miles to attend services. What church member today would walk from ten to twenty miles (coming and going) to attend Sunday morning services? Anniversaries, such as the one we are about to celebrate, if they are to be of any value, should bring out these contrasts, should stress the homely virtues of the pioneers, should restate and amplify the principles of these "original fathers" (Swedes, Finns, Dutch and English), that later grew into the fundamental philosophy of early America.

This and other publications in connection with the celebration of the 300th Anniversary of the Establishment of Civilization in the Delaware Valley should help to do this. We are happy, especially those of us who are "historically minded," that this celebration has given rise to publications of this kind.

AMANDUS JOHNSON.

CONTENTS

PREFACE
 By Mrs. Irene Fuhlbruegge, State Director, Federal Writers' Project of New Jersey

INTRODUCTION
 By Dr. Amandus Johnson, Director of the American Swedish Historical Museum

LIST OF ILLUSTRATIONS

I. THE SWEDISH BACKGROUND	1
II. WHERE THREE NATIONS MET	13
III. MINUIT FOUNDS NEW SWEDEN	18
IV. THE SWEDES PURCHASE NEW JERSEY	22
V. PRINTZ BUILDS FORT ELFSBORG	29
VI. SWEDEN RULES THE DELAWARE	36
VII. "BIG BELLY" vs. "PEG-LEG"	47
VIII. THE FALL OF NEW SWEDEN	51
IX. SETTLEMENTS ON NEW JERSEY CREEKS	57
X. THE RISE OF THE CHURCHES	70
XI. ENGLISH AND GERMAN INFLUENCES	81
XII. A PORTRAIT OF NEW SWEDEN	88
XIII. THE SECOND FALL OF NEW SWEDEN	96
XIV. THE SWEDES AND FINNS AS AMERICANS	101
XV. SWEDESBORO	115
XVI. PENNS NECK	129
XVII. THE GLEBE	137
XVIII. REPAUPO	140
XIX. PORT ELIZABETH	144
XX. FRIESBURG CHURCH	147
XXI. FORT ELFSBORG	149
CHRONOLOGY	153
BIBLIOGRAPHY	158
INDEX	161

LIST OF ILLUSTRATIONS

	Facing Page
TRINITY CHURCH STEEPLE, SWEDESBORO	Frontispiece
KING GUSTAVUS ADOLPHUS	4
Courtesy of American Swedish Historical Museum.	
AXEL OXENSTIERNA	8
Courtesy of American Swedish Historical Museum.	
QUEEN CHRISTINA	8
Courtesy of American Swedish Historical Museum.	
THE KALMAR NYCKEL	18
From *The Majestic Delaware*, by Francis Burke Brandt.	
JOHAN PRINTZ	30
Courtesy of American Swedish Historical Museum.	
SWEDISH CHEST	44
Owned by Mrs. Louise Sinnickson Grey.	
SWEDES CREEK	58
RACCOON CREEK AT BRIDGEPORT	64
REPAUPO	64
TRINITY EPISCOPAL CHURCH AND GRAVEYARD, SWEDESBORO	76
SITE OF MAURICE RIVER CHURCH	84
NOTHNAGLE HOUSE	84
RACCOON AND PENNS NECK CHURCH REGISTER	88
SILVER COMMUNION SET, TRINITY CHURCH, SWEDESBORO	94
NICHOLAS COLLIN	100
Courtesy of American Swedish Historical Museum.	
CROWN PRINCE GUSTAF ADOLF OF SWEDEN	104
SWEDISH LOG CABIN DETAIL	108
SWEDISH TERCENTENARY STAMPS	108
"OLD MAIN," UPSALA COLLEGE, EAST ORANGE	112
TRINITY CHURCH INTERIOR, SWEDESBORO	120
SWEDESBORO, KINGS HIGHWAY	126
ST. GEORGE EPISCOPAL CHURCH, CHURCHTOWN	132
GLEBE, OR PARSONAGE FARM, NEAR WOODSTOWN	138
PORT ELIZABETH	144
FRIESBURG LUTHERAN CHURCH	148

The Swedes and Finns in New Jersey

I

THE SWEDISH BACKGROUND

SWEDEN was a latecomer in the European quest for empire in the New World. Between 1600 and 1625 several other nations had made substantial starts toward trade and colonization in North America. Sweden's task as a potential colonial power was to overtake if not outstrip her predecessors in the New World. Her effort to do this was the short-lived colony on the Delaware River, whose brief history was exciting and dramatic enough to win it a 300-year memory.

The reasons for Swedish interest in American colonization are today almost obvious. Like the English, French and Dutch before them, Swedish nobles and merchants saw ready riches to be made from furs and skins in the New World as well as new markets for home products. Similarly, the Crown envisioned greater international prestige and larger revenues from New World colonization and plunder of the Spanish ships in the Atlantic.

Despite the natural interests of Crown and commoner, the condition of Sweden in the first half of the seventeenth century presented many obstacles to carrying out a fully developed program of colonization. Colonies required vast original investments if their operators were to hope for a return; Sweden was, by comparison with France, England or Holland, an undeveloped, uncommercial country. Colonies required managers and voyagers experienced with conditions in a new country; despite its maritime tradition, Sweden at this time had no experienced explorers or colonizers. Colonies needed the backing of a united mother country; despite the strong hand of King Gustavus Adolphus, Sweden seethed with conflict between nobles and burghers; and the King's court was more likely to be a battlefield in Germany than a stone-walled chamber in Stockholm. Finally, colonies prospered most when the future colonists were eager to try their fortune in a new land; there is little evidence of such interest in Sweden at this time.

Why then did Sweden, with so many factors opposing the venture at colonization, make an effort to revive her maritime tradition? Swedes had taken a large part in the romantic and dangerous voyages of the Vikings between 800 and 1000 A. D. Possibly there had even been Swedes on Lucky Lief Ericson's ship when he happened upon the grape-covered coast which he called Vineland. Compared with Russia to the east, barely stirring in its prolonged medieval slumber, and with Poland to the south, bloody and destitute from its provincial wars, Sweden qualified as a nation with an international attitude.

A further comparison with her neighbors helps to explain Sweden's action at this time. The internal troubles of Gustavus Adolphus were as nothing compared to the incessant strife in the kingdoms of Norway and Denmark. Sweden's few cities still outnumbered those of other Scandinavian countries. Her army and navy were the best in her section of Europe, and her ambassadors had outdistanced those of Poland, Russia and other adjoining countries. The hand of the House of Vasa had, in a word, made Sweden the most progressive nation among its neighbor states.

Sweden, then, at the opening of the second decade of the seventeenth century was beginning to push south into continental Europe for markets and political influence, much as Russia was destined to do a century later under Peter the Great. Four years before Gustavus Adolphus came to the throne in 1611, a commercial company had been chartered at Gothenburg to gain a greater measure of continental trade, but had proved unsuccessful.

The king and his wise chancellor, Axel Oxenstierna, knew, however, that they must consolidate their position at home in order to bid for a larger place in world commerce and politics. Industry and trade were encouraged; returning veterans of the army were given land grants on which vast forests were cleared to provide charcoal for

THE SWEDISH BACKGROUND

smelting; new land was opened up to agriculture; and Belgian iron workers were imported to supervise the ore production of the country. They came to the new port of Gothenburg, founded in 1598 for more direct western trade routes by Charles IX, and helped to build that city's commercial importance. At the same time, domestic artisans were encouraged to utilize Swedish wool for home textile manufacture. Politically, Gustavus Adolphus enlarged the Riksdag, or Swedish parliament, to admit peasants, limited somewhat the privileges of the nobility and opened civil and military positions to all citizens.

Between 1611 and 1629 the king successfully fought Denmark, Russia and Poland. These continental expeditions brought more and more Swedes into contact with Central Europe. The soldiers' minds, like those of their warrior-king, began to conceive of the Fatherland as the great empire of the North. Sweden at this period included, in addition to its present-day territory, Finland, Estland (Esthonia) and Latvia (then called Ingermanland), and was the largest Scandinavian country.

With the new blood of increased trade and military triumph in its veins, Sweden in the middle of the third decade of the seventeenth century was undoubtedly fertile soil for the plans of many colonial promoters—men who were touring the courts of Europe to stir interest in the trade and territory available through the discovery of the New World and quicker routes to India.

No promoter, however, had to inform Gustavus Adolphus and Oxenstierna of the fabulous wealth already acquired by the more westerly nations. Sweden had been watching for generations the rise of Catholic Spain and Portugal on the gold extracted from Mexico, Peru and Brazil, and on silk and spices from the East. Ministers and merchants also knew of the English settlement at Jamestown, Virginia, in 1607, and at Plymouth in 1620. And Holland, the continental country with which Sweden had had the most traffic, had only recently (1623) built Fort Nassau on the Delaware River. Sweden, bidding for the rank of a major power alongside England, Spain, Portugal and France, needed only the right man to translate her interest in a broader horizon into action.

Holland supplied that right man. To Gothenburg in 1624 came Willem Usselinx, founder of the famous, powerful Dutch West India Company, bitter at having failed to receive "what he considered his just dues" from the States-General of the Netherlands, eager to see the new port the Swedes were building on the Kattegat Sound, and hopeful of obtaining Crown support for a new trading company. Gustavus Adolphus was fortunately in Gothenburg at the time of his arrival and Usselinx shortly obtained a hearing.

The speed with which Gustavus Adolphus adopted the plans of the Dutch promoter is significant in judging his attitude toward New World enterprise. No more than two months could have elapsed between Usselinx's 6-hour audience and the issuance of a charter on December 21, 1624. Although foreign trading companies were no novelty to Sweden, the South Company, as it was to be called, was by far the most ambitious yet organized. Usselinx received a commission "to establish a General Trading Company for Asia, Africa, America and Magellanica." Sweden's official interest in American trade began with this charter.

The grand plan promptly failed. Despite exhortations in Sweden by the King and the Oxenstierna family and solicitation up and down the coasts of the Baltic Sea and the Gulf of Finland by Usselinx himself, subscriptions were considerably below expectations and collections even more meager. In the summer of 1627 the directors of the struggling company sent Usselinx to the battlefields of Prussia to urge the King to pay his own first installment of 115,-000 dalers (approximately $115,000). The needs of his soldiers seemed more immediate to the King than those of the embryonic trading company, and Usselinx failed to collect.

Despite default by the King and many others, some funds were collected. In the promoter's absence, the directors of the company realized that their monies were not

Gustavus Adolphus (1594-1632), *King of Sweden*

THE SWEDISH BACKGROUND

sufficient for a long voyage. Consequently they began to negotiate for Russian trade. In 1628 they built a glass factory at Gothenburg and a ropewalk at Norrköping. With his dream of far-flung expeditions reduced to domestic manufacturing, Usselinx regretfully obtained his release from the King in 1629. The prophetic shadow of insufficient capital had already begun to lengthen over Swedish plans for increased world trade.

In the same year Gustavus Adolphus and his minister turned their attention to strengthening the navy and merchant marine by forming a ship company. Into its coffers were drained the financial assets of the South Company and later the ideas of Usselinx. In 1631 the company sent six ships to trade in hostile Spain. The vessels were commandeered by King Philip of Spain and ultimately sailed to the West Indies in the service of the Spanish Crown.

The ubiquitous Usselinx had meanwhile recovered from the collapse of the South Company and in 1632 returned to Sweden. This time his plans were for an international mercantile company. Having already interested Protestant cities of Germany in the scheme, he quickly won over their ally, Gustavus Adolphus, who again expressed great hope for realizing Sweden's share of New World commerce.

Failure, however, dogged Usselinx. Before negotiations were completed in 1632, Gustavus Adolphus, after 3 years of triumph and conquest as the champion of the Protestant cause on the battlefields of Germany, was slain at the Battle of Lützen. The results of his death as well as his German campaign were cardinal factors in the history both of Sweden and of New Sweden.

The immediate effect upon the burgeoning New South Company was disastrous. Although chartered and supported by Oxenstierna, who became the regent for 6-year-old Queen Christina, Usselinx's new company met the same fate as the 1624 organization; subscriptions were below expectations and the defeat of Swedish armies in the field in 1634 killed the plans of the promoters in Sweden as well as in Germany.

Along with the mantle of authority, Oxenstierna assumed the task of carrying forward Gustavus Adolphus' plans and hopes for the development of Sweden. The dead King had left the chancellor a well-plowed field in which to work. Not only had the military might of the nation made it respected throughout western Europe, but also the King's foreign campaigns had aroused the Swedes' interest in lands beyond their borders. Inextricably bound up with Gustavus Adolphus' ambition to play the role of protector of the Protestant faith in Europe was the establishment of a powerful Sweden. This implied the enlargement of the limits and prestige of his own domain. As Dr. Andrew Stomberg observes, "The ability of Sweden to carry on this great role was contingent upon her having a strong military organization, and *control of strategic points in north Germany and the Baltic Lands.*"

This idea of empire appealed likewise to Oxenstierna. By far the ablest statesman in Swedish history, he successfully pursued as regent the policies of Gustavus Adolphus. For 26 years he labored to make Sweden a first-class voice in the concert of nations. Perhaps the most significant tribute to this great neglected figure was that of Cardinal Mazarin, himself one of the foremost statesmen of France: "If all the diplomats of Europe were in a boat together, they would unhesitatingly entrust the rudder to Oxenstierna."

In such a man's grasp, then, was the tiller of Swedish colonial enterprise. The varying fortunes of the Thirty Years' War in Germany dimmed whatever hope of land acquisition on the continent Oxenstierna may have had. Once again it required only the proper approach to turn his thoughts of empire westward.

And once again Holland supplied the stimulus—that is, in conjunction with a Swedish stimulus. On the strength of notes held against a large quantity of copper Sweden had stored in Holland, Samuel Blommaert, Dutch copper magnate, financier and promoter, entered Oxenstierna's plans. Through the Swedish commissioner in Holland, he awakened the Chancellor's interest in Guinea as a possible market for Swedish copper, then one of the major products of the kingdom. Like Usselinx before him, Blommaert had become disgusted with the Dutch West India Company, of which he was a director, and sought new backing for overseas commerce. Unlike Usselinx, however, he had had close relations for years with Swedish statesmen and Swedish trade. Moreover, he had ready cash. This was to prove an important factor in Blommaert's success in more difficult waters than those in which Usselinx repeatedly floundered.

Early in 1635 Oxenstierna visited the continent to obtain French aid against the rising power of the Catholic forces in the Thirty Years' War. On his way home he stopped at Amsterdam. His desire to improve Sweden's iron and copper trade naturally led him to Blommaert, and the meeting was fruitful. The Swedish minister listened attentively to the Dutchman's proposal for getting new markets in both the West and East Indies. Oxenstierna was so impressed that he requested regular reports from Blommaert and promised him a reward and a permanent position.

For the third time, internal strife in the Dutch West India Company helped to determine the development of Sweden's transatlantic experiments. In Amsterdam at the time was Peter Minuit, who probably knew as much about the New World and its colonization as any man in Europe. Director-General of New Netherland for a number of years, in 1632 he had run afoul of a new directorate of the West India Company and been recalled. Upon his return to Holland he sought out Blommaert. Minuit offered his services, possibly, as Dr. Amandus Johnson thinks, for colonizing Blommaert's lands on the Delaware River (purchased while Minuit was director). Minuit had had some connection already with the Delaware Valley, for in 1630-31 he had tried to settle it with Dutch, who quickly perished at the hands of the Indians.

The interests of the chancellor, financier and colonizer swiftly dovetailed into a plan to found a Dutch-Swedish company in opposition to the West India organization and to send trading expeditions to the Delaware under the Swedish flag. Progress was accelerated by the enthusiasm and support of Peter Spiring, Oxenstierna's representative in Holland, who reported Minuit's Delaware scheme to the chancellor and urged its adoption.

The entry of Minuit signalized a new attitude in these ventures, now more than a decade in the making. The ex-governor of New Netherland, a man of tremendous energy and executive skill, was first and last a believer in the colonial policy which Charles A. Beard has perhaps too narrowly called "England's colonial secret"; namely, that permanent settlements produced richer trade rewards than temporary trading posts. Dismissed by the Dutch West India Company, Minuit carried this idea to Sweden. Where Usselinx had proposed a large Swedish navy touching at half the ports around the globe and where Blommaert had originally thought mostly of copper trading in Guinea, Minuit advanced the idea of acquiring and settling land in the New World. In a memorial to the chancellor in 1635 he outlined the project and for the first time used the name *New Sweden.*

"The English, French and Dutch," he wrote, "have occupied large tracts of land in the New World. Sweden ought no longer to abstain from making her name known in foreign countries." His plan, as he had described it to Peter Spiring, called for him to voyage "to certain places well known to him, in the neighborhood of Virginia, New Netherland and other districts adjacent, which were to be occupied and called New Sweden." There is definite proof of Minuit's idea of settlement, for he proposed that suitable persons be taken along to cultivate tobacco and various kinds of grains.

When Oxenstierna had returned to Sweden and revived the flagging interest in the German wars, he turned seriously to the commercial schemes of Blommaert and Minuit. Shortly afterward he sent Spiring back to Holland with an authorization by the Council of State to engage Blommaert as a commercial agent for the Swedish Crown. Spiring held several conferences in Amsterdam with Mi-

Axel Oxenstierna (1583-1654), *Chancellor of Sweden and supporter of the New Sweden Company*

Christina (1626-1689), *Queen of Sweden*

nuit and Blommaert, and the formation of a company was considered.

At this stage of the negotiations, another plan was offered to Oxenstierna. It is worthy of record, largely because of the interesting contrast it presents with those already considered. A certain Joachim Stumpff of Hamburg, who had known of the Usselinx plans, proposed that Sweden enter into the New World trade, found colonies and "open up these places to merchants. With a few people Sweden could carry out this great undertaking, for merchants from other nations would take part in it and assume a large share in the cost." Thus Stumpff was even more direct than Minuit in linking colonization with trade. His suggestion to send a "few people" to colonize is not contradictory to the idea of a permanent settlement, for not even the English at this time sent out more than a boatload of a couple of hundred persons to found a colony.

Dr. Johnson observes that the plans of Stumpff probably had little influence on Oxenstierna. Later events seem to bear out the accuracy of this view, for not until 5 years after the first voyage is there evidence that Sweden began to think clearly and actively of permanent colonization. Up to that time, what might be termed the get-rich-quick attitude dominated the directorate.

This was evident in the final choice of the area for the venture. Peter Spiring favored Blommaert's original scheme of finding a market for Sweden's copper on the coast of Guinea. Blommaert, however, possibly thinking of his holdings on the Delaware, had been converted to Minuit's plan; they now both wanted to found a colony on the Delaware. Spiring, although he doubtless represented the general attitude of the interested Swedes, yielded when he was shown that a capital far larger than could be raised would be necessary for trading on the Gold Coast. However, he continued to hold a powerful position in the direction of the venture, and his emphasis on trade was to make itself felt.

The New Sweden Company was chartered early in 1637. The cost of the expedition was estimated to be about

24,000 florins (approximately $12,000). Blommaert and his Dutch associates were to furnish three-eighths and Minuit one-eighth. Of the half to be raised in Sweden, Spiring pledged a maximum, if necessary, of another eighth. Although the record of privileges granted the company by the Crown is no longer in existence, Dr. Johnson infers that they contained exclusive trading rights for the company on the Delaware for 20 years. The Council of State enthusiastically enlarged the original plans and voted to furnish two vessels and a sloop instead of only one ship. Blommaert, the company's manager in Holland, began to buy a cargo for trade and provisions for the journey, while Minuit, as director of the expedition, supervised the procurement of the ships. The new company soon encountered the old difficulty which had crippled Usselinx and wrecked the three earlier plans: again the Swedish members were slow in payments; and the Dutch, who probably had much more ready cash, prudently withheld their money until the agreed sum had been collected in Stockholm.

Then and there the New Sweden Company and all its grandiose plans might have gone the way of its predecessors had it not been for the personal wealth and faith of two of its directors. In Holland, Blommaert advanced the company large sums from his own pocket to purchase cloth, trinkets and other articles for the Indian trade, and Klas Fleming, a leading member of the nobility and general director of the company in Stockholm, lent money to Minuit and met the colonizer's doctor bills while he was sick.

Blommaert also had the problem of hiring a crew, for at this time Sweden's small merchant navy had few good seamen. He finally hired sailors and officers in Holland, and toward the end of July 1637 the men and the cargo and some of the supplies reached Gothenburg, the embarkation point.

Delays continued. Only hard driving by Fleming finally got the authorization of two of the government's three promised ships by the end of August. The *Kalmar Nyckel*

THE SWEDISH BACKGROUND 11

(*Key of Kalmar*) and the *Fogel Grip* (*Bird Griffon*) then lay in the harbor of Gothenburg, the only indication of their future course being the loading of the cargo. The shareholders were by this time viewing the mounting expenses critically; the long delay in Sweden meant that the officers and men had to be paid while doing nothing. Blommaert and Minuit, however, quieted the grumbling and apprehension by picturing a large profit from the trade. Significantly, Blommaert also observed—concerning the increased overhead—that "a good rich Spanish prize will be able to pay for it all." The investors had doubtless heard enough about rich loot taken from Spain's ships, homeward bound from Mexico and Peru, to envision greater immediate profit from such a snare than from the fur or copper trade. Moreover, the fact that the first expedition was a necessary preliminary risk made the Spanish prize most desirable.

No matter what ultimate ideas of dominion or colony Minuit and Oxenstierna may have had, the personnel of the first trip indicates clearly that the voyage was primarily to establish trade with the Indians and to get the lay of the land. In the midst of the vexation and turmoil which continued to postpone the sailing, Minuit had no time to worry about his future pioneers. Including himself, the first citizens of New Sweden would number exactly 26.

When compared with the 140 Pilgrims who sailed to found Plymouth, or the 105 persons who stayed at Jamestown, the number of settlers on the initial Swedish expedition makes it clear that the company expected Minuit to found no more than a trading post at this time.

And of the 26 there were few enough Swedes to found a New Sweden. A number of the soldiers were Dutch, as was, of course, Minuit himself and his relative, Hendrick Huygen, the company's commissioner, who would manage the trading. For more variety, there was a Negro slave boy, Anthony, and possibly one William Laury, the provost, who Dr. Johnson suspects was an Englishman. Again unlike most of the English, the Swedes took neither women nor children with them, and it is reasonable to assume that all expected to return to Europe as soon as the Crown or the company permitted.

Truly "a little band," the group finally sailed from Gothenburg early in November. The two little ships were badly buffeted about by angry storms in the North Sea, and early in December each was in port in Holland for repairs. By December 20, new provisions had been taken on and all was ready for the voyage. But unfavorable winds caused further delay, and Minuit added a cargo and six persons bound for New Netherland. Finally, on December 31, the *Fogel Grip* and the *Kalmar Nyckel* sailed out of the Dutch harbor of Texel into a New Year and toward a New World.

II
WHERE THREE NATIONS MET

MODERN Americans, knowing the vastness of their country, often find it difficult to understand the spirited struggles between European nations over relatively small areas of the continent during the seventeenth and eighteenth centuries. And today it seems particularly ironic that the Delaware Valley, one of the smallest of these small areas, should have been the theater of a three-cornered battle. The conflict between the Dutch, English and Swedes ended in no smashing military victory such as Quebec, but for complexity and intrigue it equaled any territorial dispute in the New World.

The zeal with which the mother countries fought for strips of land while an entire continent lay beyond can be explained by the fact that these strips controlled the back country. The Delaware Valley, for example, was the market place for the fur trade of the New Jersey, Pennsylvania and Delaware areas. Furthermore, every foot of travel cost money, and it was considerably less expensive to colonize along a river than to push into the uncharted hinterland.

The two great valleys of the American seaboard in Colonial days were the Hudson and the Delaware. By 1638 the Hudson had been established as a Dutch waterway, but the Delaware awaited the decisive grasp of a European power. When the Swedes sought to play that role with their new trading company, they ran directly into the claims, interests and efforts of the Dutch and English. Although neither had mastered even a tiny portion of the valley, neither intended to abandon it to the ambitions of another nation.

The old dream of European navigators of a water route to the Indies led to the discovery of the Delaware. The river may have been visited by voyagers of a number of nations from the Vikings before 1000 A. D. to the French in the middle of the sixteenth century, but Henry Hudson, an Englishman in the employ of the Dutch East India Company, is credited with its discovery in 1609. In quest of a northwest passage to Asia, Hudson brought the *Half Moon*, which was later to sail the Hudson River, into Delaware Bay and up the river as far as hidden shoals and tiny islands would permit. He made no attempt to colonize, but the river was known for generations by the name his Dutch employers bestowed upon it: South River.

A year later the English gave the river its present name. Captain Samuel Argall anchored in the bay and called the southern point "Cape De la Warr" in honor of Lord De la Warr, official head of the expedition on his way to take up his duties as Governor of Virginia. Soon the English in Virginia began to use "Delaware" for both the bay and the river.

The Dutch lost no time in capitalizing on Hudson's discoveries. In 1614, on the strength of further exploratory voyages on the Hudson and Delaware, they formed the United New Netherland Company. By 1620 Captain Cornelius Jacobsen Mey had ascended the Delaware beyond the Schuylkill for the company. Three years later he returned to build a fortress which he called Fort Nassau. Placed on the New Jersey side of the river near the present site of Gloucester, this was the first white colony in the Delaware Valley. Four couples and eight sailors comprised the population. Although intended by the Dutch to hold the valley against the encroaching English and French, Fort Nassau was deserted by 1632.

Meanwhile Samuel Godyn, president of the Amsterdam chamber of the West India Company, and Samuel Blommaert purchased a tract of land near the entrance of Delaware Bay. Twenty-eight colonists founded Swanendael there in 1631, but the colony was soon wiped out by the Indians.

The English claimed the Delaware Valley on the broad basis of John Cabot's discovery of North America in 1497. The original grant to the Virginia company in 1606 had

WHERE THREE NATIONS MET

In addition to the fact that King Charles was well disposed toward Sweden, there is a suggestion of evidence for the argument in the difference between the trading charters received by Usselinx in 1626 and 1632. The former granted rights to trade on the coast of America beginning at the same latitude as the Strait of Gibraltar—from the present-day Cape Lookout on the North Carolina coast south. The latter charter removed all territorial limitations and so included Delaware within the sphere of the company's activity.

It should be noted that this change occurred before Blommaert and Minuit had proposed the Delaware region to Oxenstierna; also that England had earlier attempted to establish—quite close to the 36th parallel but never below it—Raleigh's Lost Colony at Roanoke in 1587. The 36th parallel might have been chosen as the southern limit of English holdings. A change 6 years later might similarly have been the result of a new conception of the English boundary.

Obviously the problem presents endless speculation. Dr. Johnson inclines to the belief that the Swedes might have been granted either the privilege to visit English colonies in America or the right to erect trading posts on territory unoccupied by the English. Up to 1634 the Dutch had been the main traders in the valley. Dr. Johnson dismisses the suspicion that Governor Rising would have invented the story, but concedes that it might have been magnified from trading privileges to the cession of territory.

Whatever agreements may have existed between England and Sweden prior to 1638, there can be no doubt on two points: first, that Peter Minuit and the New Sweden Company were committed to establish trading posts and later colonies on the Delaware; second, that neither the Dutch nor the English paid the slightest attention to Swedish claims no matter what their validity may have been. If the Swedes were to hold the valley, it would be only by superior strength.

III

MINUIT FOUNDS NEW SWEDEN

IN the middle of March 1638 the *Kalmar Nyckel* and the *Fogel Grip* turned their noses from the choppy Atlantic into the comparatively calm waters of Delaware Bay. The 10 weeks' voyage under Minuit had been uneventful; not even a Spanish prize had been won. Adventure and gain lay right and left of the pioneers. As they ascended the Delaware River, they crowded to the ship's rail to see the shores of New Sweden.

Minuit had been given a choice between the northern and southern routes across the Atlantic. Westerly winds dictated his selection of the Carribbean course, and, for the time being, eliminated Blommaert's secret instructions to sail to the Delaware by way of Newfoundland, which he was to claim for the Swedish Crown.

It is believed that the ships first anchored at a beautiful little arm of land jutting into Delaware Bay to which the settlers gave the name Paradise Point. Minquas Kill on the west bank upstream, however, had been fixed by the company as the destination of the expedition, and there Minuit proceeded at once. Two miles up the Kill he found a natural rock landing place and anchored there, possibly directly in front of the rock where Fort Christina was later built. The guns of the ships boomed forth Sweden's intention to take over the territory, and Minuit went ashore with a few of his men to start a new chapter in the Delaware's history.

The director followed his instructions from Sweden carefully. He boarded a little sloop and sailed up the Kill to explore the region. The little company landed several miles upstream and pushed back a distance into the countryside but "saw no sign of Christian people." Thus assured of their uniqueness, they returned to the original landing place, where the roar of the cannon had brought Indians to the spot.

Model of the KALMAR NYCKEL, *flagship of the first expedition to New Sweden in* 1638

MINUIT FOUNDS NEW SWEDEN 19

Minuit and five chiefs went aboard the *Kalmar Nyckel*, and in the director's cabin the first purchase of New Sweden was made. For the customary ornamental and useful merchandise the Indians ceded to Sweden two strips of land on the west bank of the Delaware. One extended 40 miles south of Minquas Kill to Bomten's Point, while the other ran 27 miles north to the Schuylkill. Minuit had been instructed to buy land up to Trenton Falls, and there is no explanation for his failure to do so. As was customary in Colonial land sales, the western boundaries were left to the imagination of the purchasers.

When the land had been purchased, Minuit and the entire company went ashore and formally took possession of the territory in the name of "Christina, the great princess, virgin and elected Queen of the Swedes, Goths and Wends." They set up a pole with the Swedish coat of arms upon it and called Minquas Kill the Elbe. The Indians departed, apparently contented with the transaction and satisfied with Minuit's promise of a large beaver trade.

After he had chosen the site of a fort and started the men to work on it, Minuit turned to the business of trading and further exploration. The *Fogel Grip* was sent to obtain tobacco in exchange for its cargo at Jamestown. There the English Governor Berkeley explained to the captain that he had received no instructions to grant the Swedes the freedom of the port. He suggested, however, that the Swedish government make the proper application for trade with the Virginia colony. The ship returned to New Sweden, unloaded the cargo and set out again in search of Spanish vessels whose captured cargoes might make up for the loss of the tobacco.

Meanwhile, Minuit had had a far less pleasant experience with the Dutch, entrenched up the river at Fort Nassau. When he attempted to sail beyond that stronghold, the Dutch demanded to know his business and forbade him to pass the fort. Minuit refused to show his papers and insisted that Sweden had as much right in the valley as his old employer, the Dutch West India Company. Despite his protest, he returned to his settlement and probably did not attempt again to go beyond Fort Nassau. Minuit's presence at Minquas Kill was immediately made known to Director Kieft at Manhattan. His emissary shortly afterward read a formal protest to Minuit, but the Governor of New Sweden, aware that the Dutch were not strong enough to carry out their threats of ejection, unconcernedly proceeded with the construction of the fort.

It was completed in the middle of May amid general celebration at the first tangible evidence of Sweden's power in the West. The fort was located on a cape 2 miles inland from the Delaware, near the present city of Wilmington. Unlike Fort Nassau it could not prevent ships from sailing up the river, but it is likely that Minuit deliberately chose the inland site to avoid conflict with the Dutch until he had received reinforcements from Sweden. Strong enough to defend the settlers against a large Indian attack, the square structure consisted of two interior log buildings, a storehouse and a dwelling place. In naming the fort, Minuit discarded the company's instruction to use New Stockholm and called it Christina, possibly because he felt that the name of Sweden's 12-year-old ruler would have a greater effect upon morale. With the guns of the *Kalmar Nyckel* mounted on its ramparts and the Swedish colors floating from its flagpole, Fort Christina stood as palpable proof of Sweden's entry into the Delaware contest.

His instructions fulfilled, Minuit lost no time in preparing for his return to Sweden to report progress. He loaded the *Kalmar Nyckel* with a few hundred skins obtained from the Indians and the cargo of the *Fogel Grip*, and on June 15, only 4 months after his arrival, set sail for Europe. Behind he left 21 soldiers, the slave boy and the provost, to defend the outpost and to plant seed for grain; Hendrick Huygen, to continue the fur trade; and Måns Kling, to command the fort. The *Fogel Grip*, then in search of Spanish gold, was to return to Sweden shortly after the *Kalmar Nyckel*.

Minuit never reached Sweden. On its homeward voyage the *Kalmar Nyckel* stopped at the island port of St. Christopher in the West Indies. While his cargo of liquor

MINUIT FOUNDS NEW SWEDEN

was being exchanged for tobacco, the Governor accepted an invitation to go aboard the *Flying Stag*, a Dutch merchantman from Rotterdam. Suddenly the harbor was swept by a violent storm which quickly became a devastating West Indian hurricane. Before Minuit could return to his own vessel, the Dutch ship was blown out of the port and into the raging Caribbean.

For several days the crew of the *Kalmar Nyckel*, which also had been swept out to sea but had managed safe return, waited anxiously for a sign of the *Flying Stag* or its survivors. None appeared. The ship then returned to Holland, bearing the journal, letters and maps of the lost commander.

The tragic death of Minuit swept through the plans for New Sweden like the hurricane in which he perished. His vast previous experience in the New World, his innate shrewdness and tact, his tremendous zeal and energy had made him the best man in Europe to bring New Sweden to a reality. He was unquestionably an irreplaceable leader. His passing lessened Dutch confidence in the venture and threw a heavy burden upon Oxenstierna and Spiring, inexperienced in such matters, to find a suitable successor. Finally, with Minuit's death, his plans for developing the trading post into a sizable self-supporting colony went temporarily into eclipse.

IV

THE SWEDES PURCHASE NEW JERSEY

SPRING and summer are glorious seasons in the lower Delaware Valley. The tiny group at Fort Christina that comprised New Sweden in 1638 must have enjoyed to the fullest the pleasures of the New World climate. But in the late fall and winter cold winds from Chesapeake Bay blow over the same region, and snow often covers the land. Måns Kling and his men may well have shivered and thought themselves once again in Stockholm or Amsterdam.

When the winter drew to a close, Hendrick Huygen again began to pursue his fur trade with the Indians. The soldiers stretched their legs after the long winter at the fort. It is fair to assume that as the days became fine and man's natural restlessness stirred in the pioneers, they ventured out over the countryside, in search of new Indian trade or merely to satisfy their curiosity about the land.

Possibly then and there the first Swedes sailed across the Delaware "to see what was on the other side." Possibly some of Kling's men were the first Swedes to set foot on South Jersey soil. For it must be remembered that Minuit's activities were strictly limited to the west bank of the river. Certainly, as a latter-day historian has put it, "The Swedes weren't going to be afraid of a little old stream, after they had crossed the ocean to America."

Little is known of the colony's activities between 1638 and 1640. Of course, the settlers were unaware of the disaster that had befallen Minuit and confidently looked forward to the arrival of a ship from Sweden late in 1639. Trade with the Indians must have been good, for Director-General Kieft complained to the Dutch West India Company that Dutch business had "fallen short full 30,000 florins because the Swedes by underselling depressed the market."

THE SWEDES PURCHASE NEW JERSEY 23

When New Year's of 1640 had come and gone, however, without the expected reinforcements and provisions, the population of the fort began to grow concerned. The *Fogel Grip* had left for Sweden almost a year before and the *Kalmar Nyckel* with Minuit aboard almost a year and a half. The delay in the commander's return worried Måns Kling and his soldiers far more than the continued verbal threats of the Dutch. Kieft claimed in his report to the West India Company that conditions at Fort Christina were so desperate early in 1640 that he had won the settlers over to his scheme for them to abandon the fortress and join him at Manhattan. The story is given little credence by scholars.

Nevertheless, the 25 men at Fort Christina must have cheered loudly on April 17 when they saw the *Kalmar Nyckel* sailing up Minquas Kill toward the natural rock wharf Minuit had used more than 2 years before. When the first excitement of greeting a ship from Europe had subsided, the settlers realized that a new commander had come to replace Minuit.

He was Peter Holländer Ridder, another Dutchman who had been in Swedish service for a number of years. His assumption of command at Fort Christina marked an important broadening in the scope and plan of New Sweden. With him the new commander brought a few domestic animals, large supplies for the Indian trade and for the continuance of the settlement, additional soldiers, a new trading commissioner to replace Huygen, and the Rev. Reorus Torkillus.

The New Sweden Company had hoped to send genuine colonists along with Ridder. In February 1639 Fleming instructed an agent to seek people in Gothenburg who would go to New Sweden. In July he asked Oxenstierna to prevail upon the Governor of the Elfsborg district to furnish 24 young men as soldiers. He felt it more desirable to have only Swedes man the garrison because there were reports of conflict between the Swedish and Dutch at Fort Christina. Fleming also requested "artisans, such as blacksmiths, shoemakers, carpenters, bricklayers, and others, three or four of whom should be married, who should take their wives along to cook, make beer and wash for the people."

This first recorded interest of the company in planting a colony on the Delaware reflects the power of Minuit's ideas and possibly the example of English success. The plan, however, failed completely. The Governor obtained no colonists, but proposed to the Crown that deserters from the army be sent to Fort Christina along with their families. Whether any of Ridder's company was recruited in this fashion is not known. But the proposal indicates the extremity of Sweden's difficulty.

Swedes at this time had no particular incentive to leave their homes for a wilderness 4,000 miles away. The Delaware colony had not yet earned such riches that it was a topic for talk around the hearth, and Europe was then as rife with stories of dangers and hardships in America as with tales of easy wealth. The motive of owning property and enjoying religious freedom, so influential in England and France, militated little in Sweden, where an all-Lutheran population had thousands of square miles of unstaked land. Finally, the country had been bled by the Thirty Years' War; its male population had been seriously reduced, and the remaining men doubtless wanted only to return to normal lives at home, with no old thoughts of Germany, much less new dreams of New Sweden.

Despite the failure to get colonists, Ridder came with the idea of development in mind. As soon as he had repaired Fort Christina, he set out to inspect the Swedish holdings along the river. To the company he suggested the erection of a new fortress on the Delaware which "would be the key to New Sweden," instead of an inland trading post such as Christina. He also requested seed to replace that which had spoiled on the voyage, cattle that could graze on the abundant meadowland, and, most important, skilled workmen to build houses and a new fort. Ridder also intended to make bricks of the available clay in the region. On May 14 the *Kalmar Nyckel* again set sail for

THE SWEDES PURCHASE NEW JERSEY

Sweden, carrying Ridder's report to the company, a large cargo of furs, some from the Jersey side, Måns Kling, Hendrick Huygen and several soldiers.

Ridder's administration of New Sweden is notable chiefly for territorial expansion. The lands which he purchased from the Indians for the first time historically placed New Sweden across the Delaware into New Jersey. Further, New Jersey became the scene of the most important political problem faced by the colony under Ridder, namely the invasion of the English from New England on land bought by the Swedes. Finally, if as Dr. Johnson states the arrival of the English in the valley ruined the Indian trade, Swedish trappers and traders must have previously been doing a flourishing business on the New Jersey side.

Not two weeks after his arrival in 1640, Ridder bought from the Indians the territory lying on the west bank of the Delaware from the Schuylkill to the falls at Trenton, "or about 36 or 40 miles above Fort Nassau." It is also thought that he acquired the land south of Bomten's Point down to Cape Henlopen at about the same time or soon afterward.

The New Jersey acquisition occurred in the spring of 1641. Extending from Raccoon Creek south along the coast to Cape May, it was by far the largest tract yet added to New Sweden. Compared with Minuit's small strips on the west bank, the New Jersey purchase was the start of real Swedish dominion in America.

It was also the start of serious difficulty with the English. New Haven colonists had been cruising and trading in the Delaware Valley for a number of years before this time. When they sought a trading site more favorably located than New Haven, the Delaware lands had a strong appeal because of the sparse settlement and because neither the Dutch nor the Swedish forts commanded the river.

The English bought from other Indian chiefs almost the identical tracts acquired on either side of the river by Ridder. It seems clear that they were sold the west bank lands after the Swedish purchase, but whether the Swedes or English held the rightful claim to land on the New Jersey side is still a matter for historians to settle. It is hopelessly confused between conflicting Indian claims and uncertain or incomplete records. At any rate, when Ridder heard of the English plans for a settlement at Varkens Kill (Salem Creek), he sailed there to protest in person, but Captain Turner, the English leader, paid no attention to him.

By the following spring (1642), the sizable settlement at Varkens Kill was gravely damaging the Indian trade of both the Dutch and the Swedes. The former had never enjoyed the good relations with the Indians established by Minuit and preserved by Ridder, and they probably felt the English competition more keenly. Worse still, the English had established another settlement on the Schuylkill lands.

To thwart the encroaching English, the Dutch and Swedes forgot their old differences and united to eliminate the new rival. In May 1642 Kieft dispatched an armed force, probably assisted by Ridder, to the Schuylkill colony. When the English refused to leave, soldiers burnt the settlement and took the settlers as prisoners.

The allies were willing to bide their time until they felt strong enough to attack the Varkens Kill settlement. But the English there had other worries. They had settled on part of the tract granted previously to Sir Edmund Plowden, and King Charles had declared them lawbreakers and public enemies. Disowned by the mother country and threatened by enemies in the valley, the luckless English colonists wrote to Ridder that they would join either him or the Dutch, according to which one offered the greatest protection. Ironically, they meant protection against the punitive power of England.

During the course of these events, New Sweden was augmented by two shiploads of colonists. The first arrived in November 1640, only 7 months after Ridder had become Governor, bringing from Utrecht Dutch settlers who settled 18 or 20 miles north of Fort Christina. They had failed to reach an agreement with the Dutch West India

THE SWEDES PURCHASE NEW JERSEY

Company to go to Manhattan and had turned to Spiring and Oxenstierna, who, still on the search for Swedish colonists, granted them permission to establish themselves in New Sweden. Because this was the first chartered settlement outside the fortress, it is worth noting that the colonists received wide trading privileges and the assurance of religious liberty. They were placed under the jurisdiction of the Governor of New Sweden.

Two years elapsed before more colonists arrived. Klas Fleming went through the same discouraging task of hunting for Swedes to populate New Sweden. In his reports Ridder had strongly urged the sending of additional colonists. Oxenstierna desperately turned to the Finns who had settled in central Sweden, and whose destruction of Swedish wilderness had earned them the nickname "forest-destroyers." Although thousands of Finns had originally been invited to migrate to Sweden and had been permitted to burn the forests there to make the land tillable, by the middle of the seventeenth century the wastefulness of this practice had brought them into conflict with the authorities.

Known as "the roving people" because of their nomadic way of life, they seemed excellent prospects for the hard life in New Sweden. Four Finns who had been found guilty of burning forests applied in 1640 for permission to go to New Sweden instead of fulfilling their sentence in the army. In the same year Måns Kling, whose first-hand knowledge of the New World had failed to enlist his countrymen, hired a number of Finns. More were added by the government's ruling that captured Finns who could not give bonds were to be permitted to leave for New Sweden. Other prisoners were also sent off to the New World. One young soldier who had cut down six apple trees in a royal orchard chose to emigrate with his family to escape hanging.

How many Finns were among the 35 new colonists who arrived at Fort Christina in October 1641 cannot be determined, but there were surely enough to complicate the already mixed relations between the Dutch and Swedes.

Grateful as Governor Ridder was for the increased population and the added supplies, his troubles with the colony were manifold. The Dutch and Swedish soldiers at the garrison continued to quarrel, and the addition of bonded Finns probably helped matters little. Huygen's successor in the commissary had lost much Indian trade through incompetence and tactlessness. So, despite the fact that by the spring of 1642 Christina had the appearance of a prosperous community with new cottages, tobacco patches and a windmill, Ridder was doubtless not sorry to relinquish control. The New Sweden Company had reorganized after Blommaert and his Dutch associates had withdrawn in 1640, and had decided to appoint for the first time a Swedish citizen to the post of Governor of New Sweden.

PRINTZ BUILDS FORT ELFSBORG

V

RIDDER'S successor was Johan Printz, third and greatest Governor of New Sweden. His colorful personality and considerable accomplishments in the face of obstacles at home and abroad make him worthy to stand in company with the more famous English Governors, Winthrop of Massachusetts, Smith of Virginia, Calvert of Maryland; and his own great Dutch rival, Peter Stuyvesant of New Netherland. Like these men, Printz saw the prospect of empire in the New World and to realize his dream strained every ounce of his energy.

For Printz that was a considerable achievement. He is reputed to have weighed close to 400 pounds, and was not amused when the Indians, with their laconic humor in describing the white man, dubbed him "Big Belly." For the most part, Printz's military strictness in ruling the colony was doubtless the most effective method in an undeveloped land. But there was a side to his nature which was as petty as his body was large. Arrogant, choleric, dictatorial, for 10 years he ran the colony like a despot, winning a despot's successes and making a despot's mistakes.

First the solider-executive, Printz was also deeply religious man who built the colony's first church. At the same time, he was extravagant in his tastes and love of luxury; when fire destroyed his island mansion, he rebuilt it promptly with even more magnificence. His love of sailing the Delaware on a pleasure yacht made him the first American yachtsman. With the colony under his large thumb, Printz ruled it almost like a feudal barony—possibly for the colony's own good.

He seldom squandered his personal bravery on petty disputes, for he was a tactful diplomat and managed to stave off the inevitable clash with the Dutch. Yet his natural brashness and his soldier's love of battle in the end did bring the Swedes their first trouble with the Indians and crystallized their struggles with the Dutch.

His precipitous nature indirectly led to his governorship of New Sweden. He had been removed from a lieutenant-colonelcy in the Swedish army in 1640 for failing to obtain a passport when he returned to Sweden from a German campaign. Anxious to redeem himself and quick to see the personal advantages, Printz promptly accepted the post of Governor of New Sweden when the company offered it to him in 1642.

The company's preparations for Printz's voyage showed that it had learned a great deal from the first four expeditions to the Delaware. Only half a hand had been extended to Ridder to help him realize Minuit's ambition for a full-fledged, self-supporting colony. Now Peter Spiring's dream of quick wealth from boatloads of furs and Samuel Blommaert's easy talk of pirating a Spanish galleon faded into the past. The company at last realized the need for more colonists, men, women and children, carpenters, tobacco growers, blacksmiths, shipbuilders and tanners. They recognized that numerous cattle and horses, and large quantities of grain and seed, were required to develop an agricultural community. Finally, they saw that in the future the steadiest profits would come from tobacco and other farm products.

A new fillip was given to the entire venture by the purchase of two new ships, the *Fama* and the *Swan*. Animals and vegetables were obtained for the voyage, but once more people were lacking. To avoid future trouble at Fort Christina, almost all the soldiers hired for this voyage were Swedes. But offending Finns were again recruited to supplement the Swedes, some of whom were deserted soldiers, debtors and poachers. With this assorted group and the men already on the Delaware, Printz's mission was to convert New Sweden from a trading post into a colony.

His two-ship flotilla could not have promised that much to the old settlers at Fort Christina when it sailed up the Kill on February 15, 1643, almost 5 years after Minuit had first landed there. Both showed the weather-beaten ef-

Johan Printz (1592-1663), third and greatest Governor of New Sweden

fects of a fierce snowstorm. The *Fama* lacked her mainmast and spritsail; the *Swan's* rigging drooped in tatters. But once the boats docked, retiring Governor Ridder, the veteran commander, Måns Kling, and all the soldiers and colonists saw that a new sun had risen for New Sweden.

Preceded in true military style by the rat-a-tat-tat of a drum and the blast of a trumpet, Printz majestically carried his 400 pounds down the gangplank. It must have sagged as much as did the hearts of any pioneers who might have hoped for an easygoing Governor. One glance from the imperious, narrow eyes of Printz, and they knew that he meant business.

The new Governor received greeting from Ridder and withdrew to hold a preliminary conference with his predecessor and his small staff. The colonists pressed forward to welcome the passengers. Questions about the homeland tumbled over one another, and were answered by questions about New Sweden. Far into the night the small group of settlers listened to news of relatives and friends, to gossip about taxes and new decrees, and to accounts of Sweden's recent smashing triumphs on German battlefields.

The following afternoon at 2 o'clock a bugle sounded attention and a drum rolled for quiet. Printz assumed a central position and slowly produced two scrolls from which he read to the excited assemblage his patent of office and his instructions from the government.

These instructions are a tribute to the remarkable understanding that Oxenstierna, Spiring and the others had of the problems of New Sweden. The provisions are also important in view of Printz's stormy career as Governor. There were 28 paragraphs, but it is doubtful whether the crowd stirred until Printz had read the last signature on the scroll. To the settlers, who throughout Minuit's and Ridder's administrations had constantly hoped for stronger support from the government, the terms of the document must have raised the hopes for a better day in the colony.

Printz's orders were simple, explicit, inclusive. He was to rule the colony according to Swedish law and right, custom and usage; he was to preserve the Lutheran faith according to the Augsburg Confession and the ceremonies of the Swedish Council; and he was to administer justice (even the death penalty) "with the most respectable people and the most prudent associate judges who can be found in the country as his counsellors."

The instructions naturally dealt with the development of farming and grazing lands. In addition, the Governor was detailed to investigate the possibilities of a number of new sources of manufacture and commerce, notably the extraction of salt from the waves (the company thought this likely "as . . . New Sweden is situated in the same climate as Portugal," then the saltcellar of Europe), the production of wine, the mining of valuable minerals and metals, the pressing of oil from walnuts, the development of silk worm culture and the pursuit of whaling and fishing. Printz was, of course, to expand the all-important trade in pelts.

The company instructed Printz to deal carefully with the Dutch and English. With the former he should mildly but firmly assert Sweden's rightful claim to both the east and west banks of Delaware River. In the opinion of the company, the Dutch would soon seek to appropriate the west bank in whole, and he should remonstrate against their preventing the Swedish vessels from sailing beyond Fort Nassau. If the Hollanders, "contrary to all better hopes," attacked Printz, he was to "repel force by force."

Apparently no trouble was expected from the English settlers on the New Jersey side. Aware of the Varkens Kill colonists' inclination to join the Swedes, the company simply commanded Printz to achieve this objective and to assert Sweden's right to their territory. He was also enjoined to make no inroads upon the English in Virginia (Maryland) since "they have already commenced to offer Her Royal Majesty's subjects in New Sweden all kinds of useful assistance." Commerce already established with the English was to be increased.

With the Indians, who had so far been on good terms with all the Swedes except Huygen's successor, Printz was to bear himself as the bestower of civilization, the Lutheran faith and good government. He was to "understand how to treat (them) with all humanity and respect, that no violence or wrong be done them by Her Royal Majesty or her subjects."

Printz's flair for dramatizing himself had given the colony a thrilling performance. Fascinated by the energy and determination of this huge man, they watched him depart a few days later in company with Ridder and a few soldiers to inspect his province. The party covered the valley from Cape Henlopen up to Sankikans (Trenton Falls), defiantly sailing past Fort Nassau. Printz's sharp eye noted the lands suitable for agriculture and grazing and for settlement, but he was chiefly on the lookout for the best location for a new and stronger fortress.

He found it on the New Jersey side. A few miles south of the English settlement at Varken's Kill the coastline strategically jutted into the Delaware. There Printz determined to build the long-desired fortress which could close the river to New Sweden's enemies. His choice was considerably better than the suggestions of his superiors. If he had taken Cape Henlopen on the west bank of Delaware Bay, the fort would have been useless against ships which clung to the east bank. Nor would Jacques (or James) Island have been better, for it lay above Fort Christina (approximately where Philadelphia now stands), and so would have allowed an invader to threaten the inland fort. Printz's long military experience fortunately rectified one of the company's few imprudent instructions.

His decision to build on New Jersey soil gives rise to the conviction that Ridder's soldiers or traders had previously explored the surrounding country, for probably the redoubtable Printz was too much the soldier not to have inquired of the attitude of the Indians in the district. And, obviously, to have chosen the site, he must have received a favorable report.

He swept into action at once. Throughout the spring Printz pushed the carpenters and laborers who had come with him on the *Fama* and *Swan* to hasten the construction. Sometime in May the fortress was named Fort Elfsborg, after a stronghold near Gothenburg, and about the same time it was sufficiently on the road to completion to cause an unidentified foreign vessel to dip its flags before the power of the Swedish cannon which had been mounted on the walls.

The fort, which apparently was finished late in 1643, quickly became the best stronghold on the river, and the Swedes lost no time in displaying its power. Printz commanded all Dutch vessels bound upstream to anchor before its walls, and toward the end of the year David De Vries, a Dutch captain, was forced to strike his colors. Earlier in 1643 Printz had detained an English ship in the service of Sir Edmund Plowden, and, not satisfied with the skipper's credentials, had sent him under arrest to Christina.

Southern New Jersey thus was transformed by Fort Elfsborg from woodlands, known only to hunters and trappers who strayed over from the west bank, to the military capital of New Sweden. Elfsborg, extending far out into the river, was the dirk that Printz used to carve out of Delaware Valley the empire of New Sweden. The majority of the Swedes undoubtedly remained for some time on the west shore of the river, but they owed security and power to the armed projection on the New Jersey coast. How many Swedes stationed at Elfsborg cut their way into the New Jersey back country, there to establish farms, individual trading posts and trapping machinery, can only be guessed.

The only sizable colony in New Jersey under Printz's rule was the English one at Varkens Kill. Fort Elfsborg was primarily a defense post rather than a growing community. When Printz arrived in 1643, the unhappy New Englanders were on the verge of disbanding. The colonists had faced the threats of the Dutch, Swedes and their own countrymen; sickness had attacked them, and their spirit was at a low ebb. Impressed, however, with Printz's new fort near by, they decided that the Swedes offered greater protection than the Dutch and swore allegiance to the Crown of Sweden. It is said that Printz forced the English to take the oath and drove away those who would not.

Dr. Johnson believes the story has no foundation, but it is not inconsistent with Printz's rash and arbitrary record in the New World. The colony had been estimated by the New Sweden Company to consist of 60 families or 100 persons, but how many became Swedish subjects is not known.

By June 1643 Printz had made himself the unquestioned master of the valley. He had moved the capital of New Sweden to Tinicum Island, where he was building another stronghold, Fort New Gothenburg. This triangular island, which is really a part of the west bank mainland and only insular by virtue of a creek which branches at its apex, was much closer to Jacques Island, the company's original choice for a fortification. Work on the fort was slow, for the colonists were also felling trees for the houses of the new village and laying out tobacco plantations and corn patches.

For Printz himself there was being built what must have appeared a House of the Great Spirit to the Indians and an imposing dwelling to the Europeans themselves. To begin with, the gubernatorial mansion rose two stories high, overshadowing everything else on the island except the fort. Built of hewn logs, it had interior fittings of sawed lumber, brick fireplaces and chimneys, and, most luxurious of all, windows of glass. Christopher Ward, in *The Dutch and Swedes on the Delaware,* thinks it was the finest house in America between Virginia and Manhattan Island, and it doubtless was.

His household established, two forts under way and a third being repaired, crops planted and a good cargo of tobacco and skins dispatched on the return voyage to Sweden, Printz settled down to rule New Sweden.

VI

SWEDEN RULES THE DELAWARE

PRINTZ'S quickly won sway over the Delaware was almost as quickly challenged. Despite his hot temper and imperiousness, he had followed instructions and kept on good terms with both the Dutch and English. But a Governor of a less autocratic temperament would have been driven to action by the behavior of the Connecticut English who still insisted on their trading rights at Varkens Kill.

The Swedish Governor had built Fort Elfsborg to defend New Sweden's claim to the New Jersey territory—to repulse enemy ships, and to keep an eye on the English settlement nearby. Printz was worried about the English from the time of his arrival. In April 1642 he wrote to the Governor of Finland that he had "evil neighbors, especially the English."

In spite of his treatment of Plowden's men at Fort Elfsborg, Printz later made an effort at friendliness to the English by aiding Lord Plowden himself when he came to New Sweden as the castaway victim of a scheming skipper. Printz befriended Plowden and caught his betrayers, whom he delivered to the English Governor. He also sent along a bill of 425 rixdollars for expenses incurred, which the English paid. He refused to permit English ships to pass Fort Elfsborg, but Plowden at Jamestown merely protested his action.

But George Lamberton, one of the organizers of the Varkens Kill settlement, refused to take seriously the Swedish monopoly. He insisted upon the priority of the English land purchase and his right to trade on the Delaware. In fact, he had continued to do so after his Schuylkill plantation had been destroyed by Kieft and Ridder. On June 22, 1643, he presented a formal protest to Printz, claiming ownership of both the Schuylkill and Varkens

Kill lands. He then sailed 3 miles beyond Fort Christina, where he anchored to trade with the Indians.

What Printz planned to do about Lamberton is a matter of guesswork, for there is no record of a reply to the Englishman. But 4 days later, June 26, whatever his thoughts had been, Printz was forced to action.

As he came from morning prayers, two excited colonists rushed toward the Governor with a story that Lamberton had bribed the Indians to murder the Dutch and Swedes and destroy their settlements. By a ruse Printz placed spies on Lamberton's boat to learn what they could. Another trick brought him and his men to Fort Christina, where they were arrested. They were set free on the promise that they would appear at a court of inquiry at Fort Christina.

The court met on July 10. Consisting of English, Dutch and Swedish commissaries, it proved to be much more of a rehash of the old land feud between Lamberton and New Sweden than a murder trial. Printz may have taken little stock in the reported massacre and may have used it chiefly to subjugate the persistent Lamberton. At any rate, on Printz's request the English claim to Delaware lands was examined first.

The court went over the same ground that had been covered in disputes between Ridder, Kieft and the English. On the west bank Lamberton's claim was, to say the least, shaky; he argued that he had been induced to buy the tract by the Dutch commissary at New Netherland, although he knew of the Swedes' prior purchase. That official hotly swore that Lamberton "lied like a wanton rascal," and it must have amused Printz to have the Dutch defend Swedish claims so stoutly. On the Jersey side, the argument revolved around the question of the rightful Indian ruler. The court threw out completely Lamberton's claims to either side of the valley.

The charges made against Lamberton personally dealt with his illegal trading and the alleged plot to murder the Swedish settlers. Two colonists swore that they had heard the Indians talking of the Englishman's plans for a massacre. Lamberton denied it, and it was his word against that of the Swedes. The court found Lamberton guilty, but dismissed the case at Printz's request. He was, however, forbidden to trade on the river on pain of having his boat and goods confiscated.

Lamberton returned to New Haven, where he stirred up Governor Winthrop by charging that Printz had obtained confessions in the case by getting Englishmen drunk and by threatening death. The Governor protested to Printz, who immediately called a second court to clear himself. The hearing descended almost to comic opera when all the charges against Printz were denied by Swedes and Englishmen alike.

The Swedes' legal victory, supported by their military superiority over the English, disposed of the New Jersey problem for almost the remainder of Printz's administration. The guns of Fort Elfsborg not only commanded the river but also made the New Jersey back country a safe area for Swedish traders. Indeed, the east bank during Printz's governorship, although it was the site of no considerable settlement, was the scene of much routine Swedish commercial and military activity. Far more than the west bank, New Jersey under Printz was indisputably Swedish territory.

The Connecticut English subdued and the New Netherland Dutch checked, Printz turned all his energies to the development of New Sweden itself. On June 11, 1644, he completed his second report for the company, to be sent on the *Fama,* which early that year had brought over additional supplies and a few more colonists, mostly timber thieves and game poachers. The Governor's report is an excellent brief summary of the colony's remarkable progress throughout the first year and a quarter of his rule.

Fort Christina had been the only settlement in New Sweden when Printz arrived. He had dotted the map with the new capital, Tinicum Island and Fort Gothenburg; established two tobacco plantations with blockhouses on the west shore, at Upland and on the Schuylkill; and had crossed the river to New Jersey to absorb the Varkens Kill colony and to construct Fort Elfsborg. The total population had grown to 121 (25 people had died since Printz's coming), and of these only one-third were soldiers. The rest included farmers, carpenters, blacksmiths and a variety of other artisans.

Printz had had little time to experiment with the company's grand plans for salt, walnut oil or wine. Beaver skins and tobacco were still the chief wealth of the colony. He expressed the hope that New Sweden's own plantations would soon be producing enough tobacco to make it unnecessary to purchase from the English in Virginia. Of the 20,000 pounds he shipped, only about 5,000 were planted in New Sweden. Printz paid a higher rate for the Swedish tobacco because it would make the colonists more industrious and would encourage new settlement.

Corn had been planted extensively upon Ridder's advice that "one man's planting would produce enough corn for nine men's yearly food." Reflecting upon the failure of the crop, Printz observed humorously, "but I received . . . from the work of nine men hardly a year's nourishment for one man." Corn, he decided, could be bought cheaply enough from the Indians, and he turned his fields over to tobacco, winter rye and a little barley. With evident satisfaction, he wrote that "It looks very fine." Nevertheless, the food problem must have been acute during the winter of 1643-44, for in a later report Printz explains that the large number of deaths were due to a shortage of grain.

Shipbuilding, an old Swedish industry, was started not long after Printz took control. By the middle of 1644 the two carpenters had built "two large, beautiful boats, one to be at Elfsborg, the other at Christina." The Governor also mentions the use of two sloops. This rather impressive merchant marine and fishing fleet of New Sweden is further proof that the colonists moved freely up and down the river, and in doing so doubtless touched at many points along the New Jersey shore to trade or even to settle for a time.

The dark shadow of trouble with the Indians fell at great length across Printz's 1644 report. Although Minuit and Ridder apparently had avoided difficulty, Printz complained strenuously of Indian murders between Tinicum and Upland and of mutual distrust. Although presents had been exchanged and a superficial feeling of truce created, Printz manifested his concern about the Indians by asking that "a couple of hundred soldiers should be sent here and kept here until we broke the necks of all of them in the river."

The trader rose in Printz as he wrote: "They are a poor lot of rascals . . . also we could take possession of the places (which are the most fruitful) that the savages now possess; and, then, when we have not only bought the river but also won it with the sword, then no one, whether he be Hollander or English could pretend in any manner to this place . . . we should then have the beaver trade with the black and white Minquas alone."

But the soldier dominated the sweeping conclusion: "If I should receive a couple of hundred good soldiers and in addition necessary means and officers, then with the help of God not a single savage would be allowed to live in this river." He exultantly continued, "Then one would have a passage free from here unto Manathans [New Netherland] which lies . . . three small days' journey from here across the country, beginning at Zachikans [Trenton]."

The Indians of the Delaware Basin with whom Printz dealt mainly were the Lenni Lenape, an important branch of the Algonquin nation. With villages on both sides of the river, they divided into three tribes: the Minsi, the Unami and the Unalachtigo. The Swedes referred to them variously as the Renappi, the River Indians and Our Indians. About 75 miles west and north of the Swedish settlements were the Minquas, tribes of the Iroquois nation who came down the kills which bore their names to trade with the Dutch and Swedes. The Swedes purchased practically all of their land from the Lenape but had extensive trade relations as well with the Minquas.

Printz, on the whole, maintained peace with the Indians, but he had considerably more trouble than either his predecessors or successors. His relations have been a matter of considerable debate, his supporters holding that he did as well as could be expected, his detractors insisting upon the Governor's natural bellicosity as a source of the trouble. Even Printz's champion, Dr. Johnson, admits on the question of the Indians that Printz was "a warrior and looked at things from a warrior's point of view. He was of the opinion that the best way to solve the Indian question was to exterminate them."

Apparently Printz arrived from Sweden with a prejudice against the Indians. He had been here only 2 months when he wrote most unfavorably of them to Brahe, Governor of Finland, characterizing them as "revengeful . . . and clever in dealings and doings" and commenting that they were not to be trusted. This was almost a year before there is any record of Indian attacks on the Swedes. In view of Minuit's and Ridder's ability to keep the peace and the traditional pacific nature of the Lenape, it is more than likely that Printz's arbitrary nature and personal distaste for the Indians strongly affected Swedish-Indian relations. Like Kieft, who had massacred red men in New Netherland, Printz hoped that the Indians would fear him even when he was bearing gifts.

For the Europeans, however, Printz had a much higher regard. He reported his clash with the English and asked for official permission to use Elfsborg to close the river to the Dutch traders who "will not even lower their flags before the forts of Her Royal Majesty." A strange scholarly note creeps into the report in Printz's discussion of foreign affairs. Almost plaintively, for him, he asks that a Latin secretary be sent out from Sweden, "since I often receive Latin letters from different places concerning this work and I cannot properly do otherwise than to answer them in the same language, in which I do not now find myself very competent, but when need so requires I must sit and laboriously collect together an epistle, and when it at last is accomplished it is only a patchwork, especially since I have more often for the last 27 years had the musket and the pistol in my hands than Tacitus or Cicero . . . "

More important to the success of the colony and its

Governor was the request which Printz saved to the last of the report. He reminded the company that he had asked for additional men in 1643 and this time sought at least a hundred soldiers "on account of the arrows of the savages." A postscript describing recent Dutch capture of a Spanish ship revived the old idea of preying on Spain's vessels. Printz pointed out sagely how his colony was much better situated for such privateering than were the Dutch.

Printz's report was sent from a New Sweden at peace with her neighbors, in serene command. It was received in an Old Sweden at war with Denmark and Germany, in desperate turmoil. Despite what they had done for the colony, Fleming and Oxenstierna naturally were more immediately interested in establishing Swedish supremacy on the Baltic than furthering it on the Delaware. The navy was so short of ships that 2 years after the Danish War had begun, the old *Kalmar Nyckel* and the *Fama* were fitted out for active war service. Worse even than the fact that Sweden could spare no ships for New World voyages was the death of Fleming by a stray Danish bullet in June 1644. Thus, at the very time Printz was requesting more colonists and supplies, New Sweden lost one of its strongest and most understanding advocates.

Throughout 1645 the colony waited in vain for another ship from Gothenburg. Trade with the English and Dutch continued, cattle bought in New Netherland grazed on the fine Delaware pasture lands, tobacco patches developed into large fields, more houses were built, grain grew and was harvested. By the fall, however, lack of merchandise from Sweden began to curtail the Indian trade. In his baronial estate on Tinicum Island, the Governor thought grimly of his winter in New Sweden. Yet, despite the failure of the company, Printz and the colony could face the winter with a large store of corn purchased from the Indians and their own grain and hay stacked or put into sheds.

Then, a month before the Christmas holidays, a tragic accident completely destroyed everything but a barn on

Tinicum Island. The gunner, Sven Vass, had been on duty as night watchman. While he had fallen asleep, his candle set fire to the fort; the powder magazine exploded and the flames rapidly burnt the storehouse, Printz's mansion and the homes of the colonists. They were cut off from the mainland until March and suffered considerably from lack of food and proper shelter.

The indomitable Printz immediately rebuilt his residence in even greater splendor, court-martialed the unfortunate Sven Vass (who was later returned to Sweden in irons), erected a new fort, and encouraged the settlers to build new homes. Nevertheless, conditions in the colony were serious. Trade was curtailed by bad weather as well as by the lack of supplies, and the forsaken Swedes were growing more restless day by day.

By August Printz had neither money nor beaver skins to buy necessities from a Dutch trader and had to give him a draft on a Dutch member of the company. To make matters worse, the crops were extremely poor that fall, and Huygen, who had returned, was sent to Manhattan to obtain rye for seed. The erection of a new mill and two nearby blockhouse, patriotically named Mölndal and Vasa, constituted the colony's progress as the morale continued to sink.

By the end of September the colonists were apprehensively facing another winter. But on October 1 a vessel flying the blue and gold flag of the mother country was sighted on the Delaware. The long wait of more than 2 years was over when the *Gyllene Haj* (*Golden Shark*) dropped anchor at Christina. Not only had Peter Spiring and the company encountered exceptional difficulties (even with the Danish war at an end) in launching the voyage, but also the trip itself had taken longer than any previous one to New Sweden. For 5 months the little boat had battled its way across the Atlantic. The passengers hardly qualified as rescuers of the stranded colonists. "The master of the ship, the mate and all the crew, except one man, were sick, so that according to their report, they would have all been lost if they had not reached land when they did."

The *Gyllene Haj* brought only a few additional colonists in response to Printz's plea for large reinforcements. But it did bring corals, axes, knives, plates and an assortment of trinkets for the beaver trade which Huygen immediately made use of. The Dutch, however, had captured much of the business and Swedish recuperation was slow.

Disappointed at the little benefit he had received after so long a wait and chagrined by the Queen's refusal to permit him to resign (no suitable successor had been available), Printz wearily prepared another report to be carried back to Sweden on the *Gyllene Haj's* homeward voyage. Some colonists returned to Sweden and the lieutenant, Johan Papegoja, also went back to make an oral report and to ask for more colonists.

Printz's 1647 report often calls the company's attention to specific requests made 3 years earlier; the same difficulties, lack of man power, administrative tangles and relations with other nationalities, remained unsolved. In particular, Printz sought instructions about the Dutch, who were not only destroying Swedish trade but also "stirring up the savages to attack us and buy land from the savages within our boundaries." In conclusion Printz again asked to be relieved of his duties.

Looking forward to his release, the Governor turned again to the vexing problem of the ever-encroaching Dutch. Since 1645 they had attempted to obtain additional land on the west bank of the river. Printz had driven them from the Schuylkill in 1645, and in the following year had destroyed their buildings in the Wicacoa (Philadelphia) section. The blockhouse which the Swedes had already built on the Schuylkill was sufficient protection only against Indians. Realizing that the Dutch would return, Printz decided to build another fort to hold the river. Finished early in 1647, Fort New Korsholm gave Printz control of the Schuylkill. He must have been quite aware of its importance, for as commander he appointed Måns Kling, the oldest soldier in the colony. The Dutch had only 20 men at Fort Nassau, and New Netherland could spare nothing but angry words to combat the Swe-

Swedish Chest, seventeenth century, showing complicated lock mechanism

dish. With the completion of his fourth fort, Printz was more than ever the lord of Delaware Valley.

In his own domain the Governor was less happy. Like himself, his soldiers and officers were anxious to return to Sweden. The Dutch had seriously crippled the beaver trade, and the high hopes for tobacco growth had vanished in small crops. Failure of the company and the government to keep a constant supply of trading articles flowing across the Atlantic had gradually converted New Sweden from a potentially commercial colony into a primarily agricultural one. Grain and Indian corn were the chief products, but corn was still bought at times in Manhattan. A few new houses went up in 1648, but lack of support from home had dampened the enthusiasm of the settlers, except the freemen who were reported to be prosperously raising crops.

In January 1648 the eighth expedition arrived in New Sweden. When the *Swan* docked, Printz received a twofold disappointment. He was to continue as Governor, and again only a handful of colonists had been sent. Papegoja apparently had striven diligently to obtain settlers, but, despite encouraging letters from friends and relatives in New Sweden, the people of the mother country were still uninterested in the colony. An especially large cargo helped somewhat to allay Printz's regrets. Probably the largest single item on board was an enormous brewing kettle, the first to be brought to New Sweden. It is believed that a brewery was started shortly afterward which provided large quantities of ale for the colonists.

For the new arrivals Printz bought new territory, the island Mekekanchkon near Trenton Falls. But when the *Swan* set sail for Sweden in May 1648 it took with it Måns Kling and many of the most experienced members of the garrison. A list compiled about this time contains only 79 male names, whereas there had been a total population of 183 in 1647 and 121 in 1644.

The sailing of the *Swan* actually closes an epoch in the brief history of New Sweden. It was the last boat to arrive under Printz's administration. It turned its prow away from a colony and a Governor securely in command of Delaware Valley. When the next ship was to arrive in 1654, the company's long neglect would have taken its toll on New Sweden. Trade would have been reduced to a meager bit, the colony would be rent by internal dissensions, and the Dutch would be threatening to overcome the Swedish altogether. Printz's keen mind saw much of this on the wall of the future, and undoubtedly the heaviest cargo borne home by the *Swan* was his very real fears for the welfare of New Sweden.

VII

"BIG BELLY" vs. "PEG-LEG"

IN the seesaw battle for power on the Delaware, the Swedes had thus far bested the Dutch. Printz had required them to strike their flags before Elfsborg, had thwarted attempts to increase their settlements on the Delaware beyond the ineffective Fort Nassau, and waited only for authority from Sweden to use Fort Elfsborg's arms to keep them off the river entirely.

The summer of 1647, however, ushered in a new era in the struggle. To New Netherland as director came a man who matched Printz for boldness, steadfastness of purpose, and forthrightness. If Printz lumbered with the power of an elephant through New Sweden, then one-legged Peter Stuyvesant stumped with the nervous energy of a rhinoceros around New Netherland. Sweden had instructed its Governor not to yield an inch of properly purchased Swedish soil; the Dutch West India Company had commissioned its director to halt the Swedish usurpation of the river. Both were men trained to carry out their superiors' charges faithfully; and in Stuyvesant, Printz for the first time had a foe worthy of his diplomatic and military talents.

The clash between the Governors came first in 1648 when Stuyvesant authorized the building of Fort Beversreede on the Schuylkill. Printz hurriedly dispatched a body of soldiers who insulted the Dutch by cutting down the trees in front of the fort and destroying the fruit. Printz ordered the Dutch off his land and when they refused, rendered their fort useless by erecting a blockhouse directly in front of the Dutch structure which completely shut it off from the river. The weak force at Fort Nassau appealed to New Amsterdam against Printz, who was charged with having "locked the river for himself." In the plaintive words of the correspondent from Fort Nassau, Printz had not left enough land on the Schuylkill "to make a little garden in the Spring."

The first encounter had quite evidently been a victory for Printz. Stuyvesant adopted a Fabian policy, and for more than 2 years the Swedes were left in control. In the summer of 1650 he even abandoned Fort Beversreede, which had never been more than a bluff met by a superior bluff.

The real battleground now shifted to the offices of the New Sweden Company and the Dutch West India Company. And ultimately the fate of New Sweden was sealed in Stockholm and Gothenburg, just as Stuyvesant's triumph was made possible in Holland itself. Both Governors sensed that the lull preceded a severe and decisive conflict over the Delaware and exhorted their superiors to send them adequate equipment.

Printz got almost nothing. A heavily laden boat sent out in 1649 had been lost in a storm. When Stuyvesant politely but not without satisfaction informed Printz of the catastrophe, the Swedish Governor promptly requested more soldiers if he was to continue to hold his advantage over the Dutch. No word issued from Sweden.

As Stuyvesant watched the Swedish colony become weaker during the early part of 1651, he determined to take a strong stand. He felt on firm ground legally, for the Dutch claimed the Schuylkill by purchase in 1633. Although the Swedes insisted that their purchase of 1640 superseded this because the Dutch had not paid for the land, Stuyvesant felt secure because in 1648 the Dutch had revived the old title at a meeting with Indian sachems who contentedly ceded the territory to the Dutch. Further, the Dutch Governor knew that Printz had only 80 or 90 men at his command. Affairs in New Netherland were quiet, and Stuyvesant prepared to assert his authority in the Delaware.

His first effort was scarcely overwhelming. In May an armed Dutch ship sailed past Fort Elfsborg and anchored below Fort Christina, closing the river. Printz hastily threw cannon, ammunition and people aboard a little sloop and sailed out to meet the Dutch. Stuyvesant had instructed his captain not to provoke hostilities, and in the face of the Swedish force he withdrew. "And thus," Printz wrote to Oxenstierna, "we secured the river again."

But not for long. The May foray had been a test, and little more than a month later the Dutch Governor gave New Sweden a real scare. Abruptly and secretly he marched 120 men overland to Fort Nassau, where he was met by ships also carrying soldiers. While his boats were cannonading menacingly on the river, the wily Stuyvesant concluded a deal with Indian chiefs for land below Fort Christina, which the Indians alleged had been sold to the Swedes by an unlawful owner.

Printz protested. Stuyvesant ignored him by landing 200 soldiers at the west bank between Christina and Elfsborg, where he began the erection of Fort Casimir. Printz put 30 men on his sloop but was powerless to do more than watch the Dutch render his haughty fort useless.

He withdrew the garrison from Elfsborg and, for practical purposes, wiped clean the official relationship between New Sweden and New Jersey. The remainder of the drama was to be played on the west bank. Printz stubbornly fortified himself as strongly as he could at Fort New Gothenburg on Tinicum Island, probably adding to it the strength of Fort New Korsholm and the Mölndal blockhouse.

Stuyvesant had ruthlessly broken the dagger which had been Printz's pride and protection. Dutch records claim that the two Governors promised to maintain neighborly relations, but Swedish accounts state that Printz doughtily told Stuyvesant that "as soon as some succor arrived he would try to gain possession of the fort." Printz knew well that a strongly fortified place on the Jersey shore would be a match for Fort Casimir. It is more likely that in the conference held between the two Governors, Printz blazed defiance at Stuyvesant and thundered his future vengeance, when aid should come from the mother country.

None had come for more than 3 years. And throughout the remainder of 1651 and all of 1652 none was to come. Internal affairs in New Sweden grew steadily worse.

The Indian trade was completely dissipated; the colonists, although in good circumstances, were discouraged by the absence of any word from home; and, to make matters worse, the Indians were growing more unruly. In August 1652 Printz again demanded men, money and supplies, but he got no reply. Finally, the redoubtable Governor himself, ill in body and deeply wounded in pride, was faced with what amounted to an insurrection in his own colony. Twenty-two soldiers and settlers accused him of tyrannical, unjust conduct and demanded the release of a Finn, imprisoned for some minor offense.

All the gall which the proud Printz had been forced to swallow burst forth from him. In a furious rage he arrested the ringleader of the objectors, charged him with treason, and after a trial hanged him. It was a bold stroke, for Printz realized by this time that the restless garrison was no longer loyal to him. Weary of the turmoil during the many years he had unwillingly continued as Governor and completely disgusted with his treatment by the New Sweden Company, Printz resolved to go home.

He had been Governor 10 years, had wrung power and prestige out of the colony, in spite of frequent indifference and lack of sympathy of his superiors, had watched New Sweden spread over the Delaware to cow the English and the Dutch, and now he ruefully saw his rivals poised on their strategic capes, in complete domination of his New Sweden. It was too much for the soldier's heart and the soldier's pride. In October 1653 he turned over command to his lieutenant, Papegoja, who had become his son-in-law, and took his wife and four children, Huygen, and more than a score of settlers to New Amsterdam. From there he boarded a Dutch ship and turned his broad back forever on New Sweden.

VIII

THE FALL OF NEW SWEDEN

AS New Sweden speeded toward disaster, the New Sweden Company and the Crown exerted their greatest efforts to establish a sizable population on the Delaware. The company was moved by continued financial failure, and Queen Christina was stirred by the loss of prestige in yielding to the Dutch. The joint action, however, produced only a pathetic last flash in the fortunes of New Sweden.

During Printz's exhortations for aid from 1649 to 1652, the company had been undergoing serious organizational difficulties. The Queen finally placed its management in the hands of the Commercial College of Sweden; it was not, however, until Eric Oxenstierna, son of the great chancellor and director of the college, returned to Sweden in the summer of 1653 that the new management made any real attempt to improve the colony.

Supported by the Queen, who insisted upon sending a large number of colonists and directed the war department to furnish ammunition for the colony, Oxenstierna plunged into the preparations for an expedition with an enthusiasm worthy of his father. For the first time since 1638, Swedes were reported anxious to go to New Sweden, but since their number was still insufficient, additional soldiers and laborers were hired. All in all, the staggering total of 260 colonists, more than four times the number in New Sweden, embarked on the royal ship *Orn* (*Eagle*) in January 1654.

The saviors of New Sweden were under the command of Johan Rising, whom Oxenstierna had known as a capable secretary of the Commercial College. The company must have suspected from the oral reports of Papegoja and Printz's son that the Governor was planning to resign, for Rising was instructed to take charge if Printz was no longer at Fort New Gothenburg. Storms and disease made the voyage the worst yet experienced, and it was not until after 107 days of miserable sailing in the foulest conditions that the *Orn* anchored off Fort Elfsborg.

A hundred of the total of 350 colonists and crew had died in the terrible crossing, but Rising delayed landing them to health and safety at Christina. The prospect of a sensational capture of Fort Casimir beckoned. In even considering this, Rising was violating his instructions. The company had wisely concluded that, if captured, the fort could not be held by the Swedes and had recommended the erection of a new fort below the stronghold. The game of moving down the river below the enemy, successfully started by Printz, was to continue.

No soldier and apparently less of a diplomat, Rising was dazzled by the prospect of easy capture when he learned from Fort Casimir soldiers, who had come aboard the *Orn*, that the Dutch, now that Printz had gone, had let the fort fall into a virtually defenseless condition. He was further influenced by the soldiers' willingness to swear allegiance to Sweden.

Their report of the weakness of Casimir was confirmed the following morning. Rising fired a salute which remained unanswered because, as the Dutch soldiers explained, there was no powder in the fort. He quickly landed his soldiers and the commanding officer took possession. Against superior force the Dutch could only protest, but they made no formal surrender. Nevertheless, Rising reported he took the fort "without force and hostility," as per instruction. Unmindful of the serious consequences of his act, the director returned to his ship and sailed up the Delaware, proud that he made it once more a Swedish river.

Rising's administration is the story of the brief, swift reprisal by the Dutch which terminated in the disappearance of New Sweden from the map of North America. As Dr. Johnson points out, Casimir was too weak to be worth taking and the rebuilding of Fort Elfsborg on the New Jersey side or the construction of a new fort would have served the purpose of re-establishing Swedish power and would have avoided the Dutch retaliation which obliterated the colony.

But the new Governor's attention turned first to the colony which Printz had consolidated at Christina and Tinicum Island. Conditions had grown steadily worse under Papegoja; 15 colonists had fled south to the English, the Indians had burned Fort New Korsholm, and the few remaining settlers were eager to go to the English, the Dutch in New Netherland, home, or anywhere away from New Sweden.

The capture of Fort Casimir and the arrival of such large reinforcements raised morale, and Rising started auspiciously. The added population caused a severe food shortage, but supplies were obtained from New England and the Indians. The colonists were permitted to trade freely with the Indians instead of as employees of the company, crops were planted, cattle raising increased, courts were established and new settlements laid out for the colonists between Fort Christina and Casimir, which the Swedes had renamed Fort Trefaldighet (Trinity, because it had been captured on Trinity Sunday). With the colony headed toward a new prosperity, Rising strengthened Fort Trefaldighet and repaired Fort Christina, which had fallen into ruin. But for his blunder at Fort Casimir, Rising made an excellent Governor of New Sweden and would perhaps have had a colony to rule for many years.

Up in New Netherland the choleric Stuyvesant wrote a furious account of the seizure of his fort to the Dutch West India Company and in his usual deliberate, cautious manner prepared to avenge "the infamous surrender" of the Dutch and "the violent usurpation of the Swedes." He bided his time and let rumors of an attack flow down to the Delaware all summer. Then in September the Swedes began to pay for their capture of "the key to the river." The Swedish ship *Gyllene Haj* mistook the Hudson for Delaware Bay. Stuyvesant pounced upon the vessel and held it while he permitted the commander to journey to Christina and present Stuyvesant's invitation for a conference on the tangled Swedish-Dutch affairs. With more pride than tact, Rising refused. Whereupon the company's eleventh expedition to New Sweden was speedily converted to the use of the Dutch.

The loss of the *Gyllene Haj's* cargo and would-be settlers weakened Rising seriously, and Stuyvesant knew it. His superiors in Amsterdam were of one mind with him: the recapture of Fort Casimir alone would completely restore Dutch prestige. They were therefore amazed when they learned in January 1655 that Stuyvesant, instead of leading a conquering expedition to the Delaware, was off vacationing in the Barbadoes. Possibly he was purposely giving Rising time to weaken himself by concentration on domestic affairs; possibly the Dutch Governor wanted additional forces for the attack. At any rate, the Dutch West India Company prodded its recalcitrant Governor by sending a ship equipped with 200 fighting men. When it arrived in August, Stuyvesant was ready to strike.

He caught Rising virtually unprepared. Since the capture of the *Gyllene Haj*, he had been occupied by boundary and trade disputes with the English and by the improvement of the colony. Shortly before Stuyvesant sailed, Indians brought the news. Rising called a council of war which decided to defend Fort Trefaldighet, and powder, muskets, brandy, beer and other military necessities were hastily shipped there.

Stuyvesant dropped anchor before the ruins of Fort Elfsborg on August 29. His fleet consisted of two battleships, two small merchant vessels, two smaller boats and a sloop. His fighting forces numbered 317 soldiers and a number of sailors. This was virtually an army in Colonial America. And its size clearly indicated that it was to be an army of conquest as well as an army of invasion.

The superior Dutch power triumphantly proceeded up the Delaware. Trefaldighet fell quickly. Commander Skute would have resisted, but mutinous soldiers and threats of a massacre by Stuyvesant discouraged him from firing a shot. At Christina the Swedes innocently believed that this was the limit of Dutch attack. Stuyvesant would build a strong fort, and all would be as before Rising had

THE FALL OF NEW SWEDEN

intemperately captured Casimir. Thus their dismay was overpowering when on September 5 they awoke to find Fort Christina surrounded. While the Dutch plundered the homes and possessions of the settlers, Rising and his men held a council of war inside the fort. They decided to hold out. The Governor sent commissioners to Stuyvesant to present the Swedish claim, but the conqueror, backed by men and boats, expansively denied that the Swedes had any right on the river at all. This sweeping denial of the events since 1638 made the conference betwen the two Governors the following day mere angry charge and countercharge.

As the Dutch speeded their preparations for attack, the besieged became demoralized; some were sick, some were mutinous, none was hopeful. To resist further could mean only disaster. On the approval and advice of his officers, Rising decided to capitulate. He hoped that his warning of the serious consequences in Europe which might ensue would restrain Stuyvesant from taking the fort over. It was an empty hope, for Stuyvesant forced complete surrender at Christina and Fort New Gothenburg.

In the moment of their triumph in New Sweden, Dutch affairs in New Netherland took a sudden turn which raised one last hope of the defeated Swedes. Indians had attacked New Amsterdam in his absence and Stuyvesant, anxious to quell the savages, offered to return Christina to the Swedes and permit them to hold the territory north of the fort. The Dutch would take only the land south of the fort. In exchange for this leniency the Swedes would form an offensive and defensive alliance with their recent conquerors.

Confounded by this amazing development, Rising summoned a council of officers and freemen to consider the course of action. Unanimously the proud Swedes rejected Stuyvesant's offer. They could not accept a proposal which involved waiving Sweden's claim, nor could they promise no Swedish reprisal for the Dutch attack. Equally important was the fact that the Dutch had so laid waste the country, appropriated their provisions and slain their cattle, that they could not have survived without immediate help from the mother country. Thus occurred the paradox of the Swedish insistence upon the original terms of capitulation. To Rising and 36 others, including soldiers and a few colonists, this meant return to Sweden. To the remainder it meant swearing allegiance to the Dutch and rebuilding their ravaged properties.

With something less than the enthusiasm of a conqueror, Stuyvesant watched the Swedes leave him in control. Surely the fall of New Sweden must have weighed heavily on the old fighter as he returned to meet the Indians in the north. He had hoped to use the Swedes to secure half his victory. Instead he pondered where he would get the soldiers necessary to hold Casimir, Christina and Gothenburg. The ghost of New Sweden was beginning to haunt the Dutch as it would until New Netherland joined New Sweden in the limbo of conquered lands.

IX

SETTLEMENTS ON NEW JERSEY CREEKS

ONLY the long silent Indians and the ever silent countryside know when the first Swedes and Finns came to New Jersey. Possibly they came as early as Minuit, possibly not before the time of Ridder, maybe not even until Printz. How early the advantages of New Jersey began to beckon the settlers on the west bank is a matter of supposition rather than historical fact.

That New Jersey did beckon, however, is a fact compounded from the character of the land and the character of the Swedes and Finns. Throughout the last half of the seventeenth century groups of Swedish colonists unconcernedly reversed the traditional course of immigration and moved *eastward* across the Delaware to New Jersey. There they built not only homes and settlements but also a leading theater of Swedish activity on the North American continent. While Sweden held sway over its colony, the west bank of the Delaware had been the center of Swedish society, but thereafter Swedes in America and Sweden itself turned more and more to the settlements along the New Jersey creeks.

The reasons for the Swedish and Finnish entry into New Jersey are inextricably bound up with the topography of New Sweden, the economic life of the settlers and the political condition of the colony. While the migration could hardly be called a movement, behind it lay forces similar to those which have throughout history inspired mass migration—land, liberty and the pursuit of adventure.

Conditions in the part of New Sweden settled between the times of Minuit and Rising gave rise to all three motives. To begin with, the Swedes and Finns who had come to the New World were primarily farmers, woodsmen, fishermen and shepherds. Unlike the city folk sent by England and Holland, they were for the most part accustomed to the rigors of combatting natural obstacles and hazards. Thus the colony's quick conversion from a trade center to an agricultural community was affected by the background of the citizenry as well as by the fertility of the land.

As farmers who planted tobacco, corn, wheat and garden vegetables, the Swedes encountered the problem of finding suitable tracts for cultivation on the rocky, steep land along the western bank of the Delaware. More often they had patches instead of plantations. Across the river, however, little creeks cut through gently rolling fertile soil and ran up into rich meadows. Thither went the enterprising Swedish farmers.

The cattlemen among the colonists had a similar land problem. Their cows, hogs, sheep, oxen and horses, necessary as food and beasts of burden, required ready grazing lands. In addition to the topographical difficulties on the west bank the Swedes found a botanical handicap. As Peter Kalm, the Finnish-Swedish naturalist wrote: "Most grasses here are annuals and do not for several years in succession shoot up from the same root as our Swedish grasses. They must sow themselves every year, because the last year's plant dies away every autumn. The great numbers of cattle hinder this sowing, as the grass is eaten up before it can produce flowers and seed. We need not therefore wonder that the grass is so thin on field, hills and pastures in these provinces." Quick exhaustion of the grasses and the scarcity of fresh grazing lands on the stony west banks led the Swedes to search for new pastures. And they found them in New Jersey. In 1655 the Swedish geographer Lindeström reports that hogs were allowed to run loose all year round on the east bank.

This same Lindeström also gives another key to the movement across the Delaware. His fellow Swedes were intensive fishers and hunters. In recounting his travels through New Sweden, he comments that the Jersey creeks were "fishful" and that the Jersey woodlands had "many wild animals, fish and birds." Since Lindeström makes no comment on fish and game on the west bank, it is reason-

Swedes Creek, State Highway 25, Burlington County

SETTLEMENTS ON NEW JERSEY CREEKS

able to conclude that then as today New Jersey offered better fishing and hunting opportunities than the west bank.

Until the governorship of Rising, Swedish settlers had not been permitted to trade with the Indians as individuals. The beaver business was carried on exclusively by the company's agent. There was considerable resentment against this ruling during Printz's administration, and doubtless many an independent Swede negotiated his own deals. And the safest place, out of sight and ready reach, was the eastern shore of the river, easily gained in a fishing sloop or an Indian canoe. It is also likely that Printz's stern methods and the frequent hard times drove settlers across the river to escape domination and to search for new sources of food and trade.

Finally, it must remembered that many of the settlers of New Sweden came to the New World as bonded servants. Deserters from the Swedish army, lawbreaking Finns and Swedes, debtors, they were required to work out their freedom over a fixed period of time, usually 3 years. It is known that many rebelled against Printz's harsh treatment and fled with their families into Maryland and Virginia. It would have been strange indeed if some had not slipped across to New Jersey as well, where in the uncleared forests along the upper reaches of the creeks they were even safer than with the English, who might return them to their Governor.

The Dutch conquest in 1655 added yet another and possibly the most powerful reason for migration eastward. It is no mere accident that knowledge of the Swedish settlements in New Jersey dates to the beginning of the 9-year period of Dutch rule and that 6 years after the capture of Christina there were at least 4 Swedish centers on the east shore of the river. Only 19 Swedes immediately swore allegiance to Holland. The rest had been granted 2 years to dispose of their holdings and leave or to become loyal citizens of the new government.

Peter Stuyvesant's leaving only a small guard after the conquest of New Sweden ushered in a period of peaceful relations between the Swedes and their new rulers. There was so little friction that the Dutch did not even bother to rebuild Fort Christina. On the New Jersey side they built nothing, and there the Swedes were free to go. Many colonists had had their homes burned, their fields ravished and their cattle slain by the Dutch troops. Across from the smoking ruins around the forts they knew of unspoilt lands. In the year 1655, Lindeström in his *Geographia Americae* has a reference which confirms an old notion that there were early Swedes on Burlington Island. After describing the land north of Burlington, he wrote, "Swedes here have no trade or intercourse with savages."

Very likely then there were Swedes on the island in 1656, when, according to William Nelson, the New Jersey historian, "a Swedish vessel sailed up the Delaware and landed goods at Matinnekonk Island (Burlington Island) regardless of the Dutch." This would have been the *Mercurius*, the unhappy vessel of the twelfth and last expedition sent by the New Sweden Company to New Sweden.[1]

On this boat were so many Finns that the commander, Papegoja, who knew no Finnish, had to take along an interpreter. Dr. Johnson states that the passengers were deposited at Fort New Gothenburg. There they joined scores of their countrymen from earlier expeditions, who had become so numerous that a section above Christina had been called Finland.

Whether the Finns gave their name permanently to a place in New Jersey as early as 1660, as has been stated, and whether their settlement of Finns Point was the first permanent settlement in western New Jersey, are still questionable. It is certain, however, that Finns were among the earliest citizens of New Sweden to occupy the land between Salem and Raccoon Creeks. By 1685 an English mapmaker labeled the present Lower Penns Neck at Finns Town, and the river between the Penns Necks, the Finnish River. It is also believed that there was a

---

1. It is interesting to note that almost for the first time the Swedish people were showing real interest in New Sweden. At about the time Stuyvesant was deciding to march on the Swedish forts, the *Mercurius* sailed from Sweden, leaving scores of would-be colonists on the docks.

SETTLEMENTS ON NEW JERSEY CREEKS

settlement as early as 1661 at the present town of Pennsville.

The entire question of dating Swedish and Finnish origins in New Jersey is virtually confounded by the fact that until the English took over the land from the Dutch in 1664, there were no official records of land titles. Although specific dates prior to 1664 must of necessity be the result of inference from careful research, the case for Swedish migration to New Jersey is strong enough to warrant credence of Swedish settlements some time before official records were kept. For example, Elmer in his history of Cumberland County writes that Swedes settled "without taking title" to land in the Maurice River region in the period 1650-1665. This condition probably obtained in several other sections, particularly those referred to above.

With the establishment in 1664 of English power, which the Swedes accepted complacently, historians step henceforth on firm ground. Whatever Swedes had come earlier to New Jersey were joined by many others after the English conquest. Actual English deeds were not issued until 1677 because of the law which required a 7-year lapse between the granting of permission to settle and the granting of title. Swedish settlers first obtained permits in 1668, but undoubtedly they had been established on New Jersey soil some time before that date.

The first permit for Swedes to purchase land from the Indians was issued in 1668 by Governor Carteret to Cornelis Learson, Ole Rasen and Ole Jonson. The permit covered the tract between Big Timber Creek and Oldmans Creek, including all of the present-day Gloucester County. Within the next five years these three warrantees conveyed all their rights to Hans Hopman, Peter Jonsen and Juns Justasen, who in turn bought the land from the Indians in 1676. It was certified in 1680 at New Castle court in Delaware that these three men, their families and tenants "have seated and improved upon ye said Land for ye space of Seven Years now last past." This establishes the first legal Swedish residence in New Jersey in the year 1673.

By 1677 the three owners had begun to parcel out divisions of the tract. In that year Oele Dircks, Will. Bromfield, Juns Justasen, Lasse Anderson Colman, Hans Hopman and his two sons, Peter Freeman, Måns Justasen and Paul Corvorn were listed as the taxables in this tract, indicating considerable activity in settlement. In 1684 their title to this area was questioned by the English. Nine Swedes, including some of the above mentioned, successfully cited the original permit granted by Governor Carteret on June 25, 1668, about a month following the first session of the first General Assembly called by Carteret. The Delaware settlements were not represented until the second session in November. The Swedes who received permits in June had probably obtained them through written requests. Despite the fact that Swedes and Finns predominated in the Delaware settlements, their first representatives in the assembly were a Frenchman from Burlington Island and a Dutchman from what is now Salem County.

Swedes and Finns continued throughout the early 1670's to take possession of western New Jersey land. Some time during these years the colony of New Stockholm was founded at the mouth of Raccoon Creek, the site of present-day Bridgeport. Other settlers moved up the creek to establish Raccoon, or Swedesboro as it has been known since 1763. There were also Swedes scattered farther north up to Pensauken Creek, where they are believed to have held land before 1664.

By 1675 Finns had spread from their coastal strip up along Varkens Kill (Salem Creek), which 40 years before had been the subject of so much dispute between the Swedes, Dutch and English. And it was again to be the scene of as bitter a conflict between the Finns and the English. The Finns were clearing the pine forests which they utilized for burning tar as well as for lumber when Maj. John Fenwick and his Quaker settlers entered the territory in 1675.

Fenwick could have gone up the Kill and left the Finns in peace. But, when he had established himself at Salem,

SETTLEMENTS ON NEW JERSEY CREEKS 63

he protested the presence of a few Finns he found there and also claimed they had no right to territory around Finns Point. Furthermore, he claimed jurisdiction over all the Finns and Swedes in the section by right of purchase of the land from Lord Berkeley, the former English Proprietor.

The Finns then appealed to Governor Carteret and to Governor Andros in New York as well. Andros considered his jurisdiction to include western New Jersey, and seized this opportunity to prove it. He went further than Carteret's mere disclaiming of Fenwick's assertions; he sent an emissary from Delaware to investigate and in 1676 took Fenwick prisoner to New York.

While Fenwick was embroiled in his multifarious disputes, the English ship *Kent* arrived on the Delaware with 230 additional colonists for a Quaker settlement above Salem. The passengers sailed up the river and into Raccoon Creek. There at the mouth they spent the winter of 1677 in the Swedish settlement of New Stockholm. Conditions were so crowded that the hospitable Swedes were obliged to lay their beds and furiture in cow stalls.

The Finns had now become unwittingly involved in a complicated battle for political control of their territory. As soon as he was freed from Andros, Fenwick returned to the Delaware and summoned the population of the section, which included Swedes as well as Finns. He demanded that they submit to him and take an oath of allegiance. Andros responded by appointing a six-man commission, responsible to his court at New Castle, to administer the territory. Among these men were two future large Swedish landholders in New Jersey, Israel Helm and Peter Rambo, who had already led the local opposition to Fenwick. He continued to struggle to some degree against Andros, the West Jersey Proprietors and the Swedes and Finns until 1682, when he made over most of his lands to William Penn, one of the Proprietors.

The establishment of William Penn and his Quaker associates as Proprietors of the Province of West New Jersey brought to the colony a peace long needed for further settlement. Penn held the Swedes and Finns in high regard and, like the Dutch before him, admired their industry and agricultural skill. Throughout his term of proprietorship, until 1702, the Swedes, almost for the first time since coming to America, remained virtually free of all governmental difficulties.

Large numbers of Swedes on the west shore of the Delaware, mostly sons of pioneer families, moved across the river in the period 1680-85, and others followed to found centers of Swedish activity in New Jersey. Among the newcomers were families such as Rambo, Dalbo and Helm, whose names were to become intertwined with the history of the Swedes of the State. In 1680 Capt. Israel Helm, who had been a close friend of Governor Printz and had arrived in 1643 on the *Fama,* sold his property at Upland and moved to Thompson's Point in Gloucester County. The following year John Rambo settled along Repaupo Creek, and 3 years later Peter Dalbo and his brother Woola established their family lands on Mantua Creek. From such settlements there gradually developed in the next century important Swedish communities bearing these old family names.

These centers, of course, must not be considered as modern towns or even villages. Swedish settlers in southern New Jersey moved up the many creeks that empty into the Delaware, taking possession of large tracts of farming and grazing land, with their homes widely separated. Therefore place names in this period, such as Cinnaminson (Senamensing), Raccoon, Repaupo or Penns Neck, refer to regions comprising a number of square miles. There was usually a central gathering spot for a region, but its position was determined by geography rather than by size.

Undoubtedly the most important of these was the settlement of Repaupo on Repaupo Creek, at the mouth of which Israel Helm had established Helmstatt. Although its date of origin is uncertain, Repaupo was a popular place of settlement by 1684. In that year Andreas Andersson (or Homan), trumpeter to Governor Printz, purchased land in the region. In honor of his former **calling**

Repaupo, the "most Swedish" village, as it appears today

Raccoon Creek at Bridgeport, where *Swedes settled in the early 1670's*

SETTLEMENTS ON NEW JERSEY CREEKS

he named the tributary creek on which he lived Trumpeter's Creek. Records of 1684 also show that land in the Repaupo region was owned by Peter Erickson and Anthony Neilson, on whose property now stands the Nothnagle Log House. The region continued to grow in importance until shortly after 1700, when the construction of the Kings Highway made nearby Racoon a genuine center, to the disadvantage of Repaupo.

North of Repaupo Creek was the smaller stream known now as Woodbury Creek. When English colonists came there in 1683 they found a few Swedish families already dwelling along the shore. The Dalbo family owned land in this region, and Walla Swanson, who lived across the Delaware River, also possessed 200 acres in the Woodbury section in 1683.

Swedes had come even earlier to Pensauken Creek, farther up the Delaware. In 1682 Markus Lawrence (or Hallings) bought 100 acres of land in the region and below him Casper Fisk owned another 100 acres along the river in present Camden County. In 1684 John Hance and Frederick King, members of the Swedish Church of Wicacoa (Philadelphia), had land surveyed on the northeast side of Pensauken Creek. This was in the Cinnaminson region, where Elias Toy bought more than 100 acres in 1689 and established the seat of his well-known family.

The extent rather than the actual size of these communities led to increased Swedish participation in the administration and upbuilding of the colony of West Jersey. Large Swedish landholders lost little time in purchasing fractions of shares in the proprietorship of the colony. Peter Rambo, for example, bought one-eighth of a share from an Englishman as early as 1682. This was inherited by his son, John Rambo of Gloucester County.

The first Swede to sit at Burlington in the predominantly English legislature was Peter Dalbo of Little Mantoes (Mantua), who attended the first session of 1685. He represented the Fourth Tenth, present-day Gloucester County, or the section from Oldmans Creek to Big Timber Creek. The Third Tenth, between Pensauken and

Big Timber Creeks, continued to be represented by Englishmen, despite the many Swedes living there.

At the second 1685 session representation of the Fourth Tenth was increased to 10 members. Three of these were Swedes, already recognized as leaders in the communities, while the rest were Englishmen. The Swedish representatives were Captain Helm, Woola Dalbo and Anthony Neilson. The latter was also commissioner for regulating lands in the Fourth Tenth. These three were returned to the legislature in 1686. It should be noted that prior to their coming to New Jersey, Helm, Dalbo and Rambo had all held official positions on the west bank.

In 1686 Woola Dalbo received an appointment as overseer for that portion of the Kings Highway which was to run through Gloucester County and which was to facilitate the growth of the Province's most important Swedish center, Swedesboro. Throughout this region the Swedes were then breaking the fertile soil for the area's future agricultural excellence. Chief crops of the period were sweet potatoes, corn, grain products and truck vegetables. Cattle raising also continued to be a main source of income to the Swedish settlements.

A tax list dated June 15, 1687, for the section of Gloucester County between Oldmans and Timber Creeks, shows clearly how the Swedes had within a few years spread up the creeks of West Jersey. There was a total of 29 Swedish landowners, holding about 5,000 acres of land and 169 head of cattle. English landowners exceeded the Swedes by only 8 and their land totaled 15,500 acres. They owned, however, only 6 more cattle than the Swedes. A few English on the list owned no cattle, which suggests that they might have lived across the river in Pennsylvania and leased their property to tenants. While the tax list cites only landowners, it gives some clue to the total Swedish population of the time. Slightly later sources, however, mention the prevalence of large Swedish families and the presence of many freemen who did not own land. It may therefore be concluded that these 29 taxpayers constituted the nucleus of a sizable Swedish population, possibly upwards of 175.

SETTLEMENTS ON NEW JERSEY CREEKS

In addition to the older regions along Repaupo, Woodbury and Oldmans Creeks, the list shows several Swedes established in the New Stockholm region along New Stockholm River (Raccoon Creek). Several more had gone beyond the mouth, and the ubiquitous Dalbos and Rambos had moved up as far as Mantua Creek. Peter Dalbo with 350 acres of land was the largest individual property holder of the time, and Lacy Colman of New Stockholm possessed the greatest number of cattle, 23. The average tract owned by the Swedes was nearly 150 acres, and most of them owned fewer than 10 head of cattle. Dalbo's estate was small, of course, when compared with the 500- and 1,000-acre tracts of his English neighbors.

At the time of these developments in Gloucester County, Swedes were also settling along the creeks and coves of Salem County. The Finns had probably given their name to the peninsula as early as 1661, but they were soon followed by English, Dutch and Swedish settlers to the region now known as Penns Neck Township. By the time Fenwick arrived in 1675, several Swedes had settled up the valley of Salem Creek toward Penns Neck Bridge. They included Jacob Hendricson, John Jacobson, Peter Johnson and Andrew Anderson. Fenwick battled against these Swedes as well as against the more numerous Finns in what he considered his domain.

In 1676, during the disputes, the Erixson family was granted a patent by Fenwick for 30 acres up the Delaware River in the vicinity of Helm's Cove. A patent for 20 acres was also granted to the family servant, Henrick Eurinson. A year later Juste Anderson acquired land on Black Hook opposite Christina Creek, on the site of present-day Deepwater. Helm's Cove, however, continued to be a favorite place of settlement. By 1685 Lucas Peterson, John Erixson and Powell Powelson owned 600 acres in this region. Deeds record the arrival of more Swedes in 1687 and 1689. The first recorded use of the name Penns Neck occurred in 1692 when the executors of John Fenwick conveyed 200 acres "on said neck" to Peter Halton.

Swedes who had crossed the Delaware earlier continued to move eastward through Salem County. In 1690 Germans who came to the headwaters of the Cohansey River and Alloways Creek, virtually nothing more than a clearing in the wilderness, found there a small settlement of Swedes. They in turn had been preceded by the Dutch. In the next century this mixture formed the Friesburg Church.

At about the same time Gabriel Thomas, an English historian, mentioned Swedes several miles southeast of Friesburg in the Maurice River Valley. In his account of West Jersey, published 1698, he attested their hunting ability in a reference to "Prince Morise's River where the Swedes used to kill the Geese in great number for their Feathers only leaving their Carcasses behind them." Thomas also mentioned Cohansey River, "by which they send great store of Cedar to Philadelphia-City."

The first Swede known to have settled on the Atlantic Coast was James Steelman, who founded the Swedish settlement at Great Egg Harbor. He had dwelt on the Delaware River, probably at Tacony, until 1693, when he crossed New Jersey and made his way to the ocean front. In 1696 he was elected overseer of highways to lay out the road "from Egg Harbor toward Gloucester." He also owned land at Absequam Beach, now the site of Atlantic City. An instance of how the New Jersey Swedes spread over the State occurs in the fact that Steelman's first wife was Susannah Toy, sister of Elias Toy, who lived at Pensauken Creek on the Delaware.

The most adventurous of all the early Swedes, however, was Eric Mullica Sr. In 1673, 10 years after he had arrived from Sweden and settled in the Tacony section on the west bank, he married Ingeborg, the daughter of Captain Israel Helm, who already owned considerable land in New Jersey. After spending more than 30 years in Pennsylvania, Mullica at 61 moved into the New Jersey interior. Far down east in Burlington County in 1697 he bought a 100-acre tract of land which he cultivated in plantation style. Here he lived until at least 1704, when records refer to his

SETTLEMENTS ON NEW JERSEY CREEKS

wife as a widow. In the same year his sons, Olof, Eric and John, purchased tracts of land on Raccoon Creek where they founded the present town of Mullica Hill. Mullica and Steelman gave their names to more places in west Jersey than any other Swedes. The Mullica River was named for Mullica because he was the first white man to explore its course. In addition to the village of Mullica Hill in Gloucester County, the name appears in the township of Mullica in Atlantic County. From Steelman have come Steelmanville, Steelman's Landing, Steelman Bay and Steelman Thoroughfare in Atlantic County and Steelmantown in Cape May County.

More significant for the development of the Swedes of New Jersey at the beginning of the eighteenth century was an event in the Raccoon region. In 1702, after many years of construction, the Kings Highway reached the small settlement of Raccoon and immediately transformed it into an important coaching center on the Salem-Burlington route.

For the first time the many Swedes south of Raccoon down to Finns Point had a good overland route northward. Helm's Cove, Oldmans Creek, Penns Neck and lonely spots in the back country were no longer shut off from their countrymen to the north. The road was the instrument by which the Swedes were to be joined into a closely knit social and religious community.

X

THE RISE OF THE CHURCHES

PARADOXICALLY the Swedes of New Jersey achieved their highest development in Swedish culture after the fall of Sweden's political power on the Delaware. As they moved across the Delaware into New Jersey in the last half of the seventeenth century, they carried with them their Swedish traditions and customs. Along the Delaware's bank, up into the lands on the tributary creeks and over into the back woods country had come clusters of Swedish families whose peaceful agricultural life permitted the continuance of Swedish ways, preserved since their American inception in 1638.

The Swedishness of these colonists persisted in two major respects: the church and the home. As farmers, merchants or public officials, the Rambos, Dalbos and Toys soon resembled their colonial neighbors. West Jersey was a melting pot of Swedish, English, Scotch-Irish, Dutch and German immigrants, in which nationalities did not long remain conspicuous. But when the Swedes left the market place or field and entered their homes they spoke again in Swedish and often sat down to Swedish dishes cooked by a wife who frequently wore jackets and petticoats of skins.

Long after the men had learned to speak English and the women had begun to wear cloth frocks, they remained almost purely Swedish when they went to worship at their churches at Raccoon, Penns Neck or Maurice River. Although it had been the devout Gustavus Adolphus' dream to spread the Swedish Lutheran faith in the New World, the colonists did little more than maintain their religion among themselves. The deeply religious Swedes were, however, as prompt as the Puritans or Quakers to provide and maintain facilities for worship according to the church of their mother country.

THE RISE OF THE CHURCHES

In fact, it was through the church alone that the Swedes in America continued direct contact with their homeland. After New Sweden had ceased to exist as a colony, the Swedish Lutherans in America retained their allegiance to the Consistory and to the Swedish monarch as the head of the established church. And from the Consistory in Sweden the churches in America received their pastors and ministers. While there is no record of American efforts to alter the practice of Lutheranism, almost from the first these divines had to combat a movement to conduct the services in English. Although Swedish flourished strongly as a church tongue until about 1750, the ministers from abroad ultimately saw the second fall of New Sweden when the Lutheran churches became Anglicized in faith as well as language.

For, despite the traditional intensity of Swedish conservatism toward hearth and altar, the Swedes of New Jersey fought from the first a losing battle to preserve anything but traces and memories of life as it had been lived in Sweden; or ultimately as it was lived in New Sweden itself. By 1750 more than half of the Swedes living in the area that once comprised New Sweden were on the New Jersey side of the Delaware. An appreciable proportion of this increased population was from the west bank. New blood from Sweden itself also entered the section, as letters and visits from Colonials made the New World seem attractive to friends and relatives in Gothenburg, Stockholm and smaller places. Nevertheless, the Swedes were subjected to successive waves of considerably larger English, German and Irish immigration, which in the end not only outnumbered them but literally engulfed or absorbed them.

Even at the outset of the eighteenth century there were signs of the outcome of the Swedes' effort to preserve their identity. Politically, for example, they were like any other group in an English colony ruled by governors and agents, loyal subjects of the English Crown, with hardly a thought of their forebears' allegiance to the House of Vasa. Swedes established schools at Raccoon and Repaupo, but for the most part their children studied alongside the English in Quaker and other denominational schools.

In the fields, where Swedes had had generations of experience, they were also influenced by their neighbors. During their early years as colonists they built sheds for the cows. Later on, however, they observed that the English let the cattle roam the pasture at night. And, against the better judgment of some of the older heads, the Swedes did the same. Similarly they began to adopt English and German ways of planting and working the fields.

More important than any of these slow drains on their individuality was the natural development of widespread intermarriage. Long before church records were kept, the Swedes had begun to marry into English, Dutch and German families. And since the Swedes were, on the whole, a poorly organized minority, they did not affect the stronger group. Hendricksons became Hendrixes; Petersens became Petersons; Lutherans became Episcopalians; and, in short, Swedes became English.

Like any absorption of a people, the passing of the Swedes was a long process, marked by bitter opposition and often by valiant efforts to stem an inevitable tide. The history of the Swedes in New Jersey is the history, on the one hand, of the disintegration of Swedishness, and, on the other, of Swedish efforts to halt the fusing of races and nationalities that was characteristic of Colonial America. As late as 1770 there were many who still hoped for preservation of the old ways and for national identity.

The prime instrument used by the Swedes to bind themselves into a Swedish bloc was the Swedish Lutheran Church. Therefore, the story of the rise and fall of these churches as institutions of Swedish worship and culture is substantially the account of Swedish homogeneity in New Jersey throughout the eighteenth century. The racial core of the Swedes, in many instances these churches survived even the transformation of Swedish homes and the thinning of Swedish blood.

The most arresting proof that the Swedes of New Jersey regarded their church as the nerve center of their lives

THE RISE OF THE CHURCHES

springs from the long, heated battle they waged for religious independence from the Swedish Lutherans on the west bank of the Delaware. Desire for their own church dated back to the arrival of the Swedes on the New Jersey creeks. Throughout the last part of the seventeenth century they had followed their faith only at Wicacoa (Philadelphia) or Christina (Wilmington).

This lack was not a new one for the Swedes of New Jersey. As far back as the days of Governor Printz, they had had to depend on the west bank for religious leadership. During the 7 months' construction of Fort Elfsborg, Printz did send there New Sweden's second pastor, Israel Fluviander. When the fort was completed and only 17 men remained behind to man it, Fluviander departed for Tinicum Island. Thus, from 1643 until the fall of Fort Elfsborg in 1651, the Swedes stationed there had to depend for religious services upon the infrequent trips of the official pastors of New Sweden, John Campanius (Holm.) and Lars Lock. Campanius not only spread the Lutheran faith by considerable missionary work, but also translated the catechism into Indian dialect. In doing so he was either contemporary with or prior to John Eliot, the Massachusetts missionary who is generally given credit for having first carried on Protestant missionary work among the Indians of the continent.

As they began to migrate to the east bank of the Delaware and to isolate themselves throughout the creek country, the Swedes realized the need for an independent church. In 1677 Wicacoa church was founded and to it went most of the New Jersey Swedes settled north of Raccoon Creek. Those on the south side of the creek continued to worship at Christina down the river. There was still the centrally located church on Tinicum Island which Printz had built in 1643.

Had this accessible church been built up into a parish with regular services, there might never have occurred the violent break between the Swedes on the east and west sides of the Delaware. But since the Swedes on the west were spreading up and down the river away from the old capital of New Sweden, such a move would have been largely for the benefit of the New Jersey Swedish Lutherans. And from 1690 on, there was little disposition for cooperation.

For the New Jersey Swedes the simple enterprise of going to church had become endowed with all the elements of a dangerous adventure. The several miles to the river or creek frequently had to be covered on foot along trails and paths newly cut through the woods. At the water's edge there awaited the crude, open flatboats that were often buffeted by winds sweeping up from the bay, tossed by wild freshets in spring and fall and locked in midstream by ice floes in wintertime. Grumblings issued from the New Jersey colonists from the first time they had to recross the river to go to church. But it did them no good.

Accordingly, when the Quakers were followed into West Jersey by settlers of other faiths, notably Church of Englanders, Baptists, Presbyterians, German Lutherans, Moravians, and later Methodists, the unchurched Swedes turned to ministers of kindred faiths. Such defection, natural as it was, apparently worried the Christina parish, for it had occurred in spite of the fact that four of the seven church board members were New Jersey Swedes. When both west bank churches decided to erect new buildings toward the end of the century, thereby permanently locating out of reach of the New Jersey members, the long discontent broke almost into rebellion.

Pastor Eric Björk of the Christina Church unsuccessfully tried to placate the angry parishioners by allowing Hans Stålt, who had just been hired as schoolmaster at Racoon, to hold services. His meetings were the first semblance of an independent church body in New Jersey, but the Racoon people thought their numbers and needs deserved far greater recognition.

These earnest farmers, sincerely seeking an independent place of worship close to their homes, ironically turned in their plight to one of New Sweden's most colorful adventurers. Lars Tollstadius was one of those bold, daring personalities out of whose doubtful characters issue good deeds and fascinating history. He dwelt in New Sweden less than 5 years, but during that time he was the center of incessant strife with the ecclesiastical authorities and the cause of tumultous wrangling between the Swedes on both sides of the river. The river itself claimed him in 1706 either by suicide or accident, but before he perished the stormy Tollstadius had given the New Jersey Swedes their first church.

He did so with a superb disregard of church discipline. Lacking even the slightest documentary proof that he was an ordained minister, Tollstadius came to the Delaware Valley in July 1701 against the authority of the Swedish Consistory. He insinuated himself into the confidence of the ailing pastor Andrew Rudman at Gloria Dei Church (Wicacoa); as an assistant he preached and catechized children but did not administer the offices of the church.

Tollstadius had moved with speed because he knew that Andreas Sandel, Dean-Designate of the Swedish Church in America, was on his way to relieve Rudman at Gloria Dei Church. This dignitary had warned Tollstadius in Europe, where the latter had already earned an unsavory reputation, to keep out of the Delaware region if he must go to America. Therefore, the young man sought to entrench himself with Rudman and his parish against Sandel's certain disapproval.

When the Dean arrived in March 1702 he asked Tollstadius to leave the country and secured him a passport. Instead of departing in disgrace, the would-be minister crossed over to New Jersey. There he stayed with friends on Raccoon and Mantua Creeks and began his master work in the New World, the establishment of his own church.

To keep the peace, Sandel permitted him to remain there on condition that he limit himself to instructing the children. Instead, Tollstadius flung down the gauntlet to both the Dean and Björk at Christina by preaching sermons. And his sermons were plainly rebellious, if not revolutionary. To the willing ears of the Jersey Swedes he spoke strongly of the need for a church on the east side of the river—with himself as minister, to be sure.

Tollstadius had seen the need. And Tollstadius had done something about it. The Swedes of New Jersey were already equipped with a preacher, albeit a bit spurious, and no ecclesiastical authority could dam the break of the New Jersey colonists from the Christina and Gloria Dei Churches. When Tollstadius began to attract Swedes south of Raccoon Creek to his scheme, Björk renewed his protests to Sweden against the upstart. Pastor Rudman was too sick to care much about the proposed raid on his parish, and Dean Sandel was too busy with the duties of his office, which carried him the length of the Delaware Valley.

Björk's letters to Sweden brought no replies. He had some small comfort when the Jersey members of his board joined him against Tollstadius. But, for most of the Swedes, the errant young preacher was a Moses in the wilderness. Sandel could disapprove, Björk could storm that the decreased revenue would further impoverish him; the Swedes of New Jersey would yet have their own church.

They had it by the fall of 1703. Before a rude altar, in a log building at Raccoon, the self-styled pastor was at last able to ascend his own pulpit and preach one of the lengthy sermons so much in vogue at the time. The sermon signalized the declaration of independence of the New Jersey Swedes from their fellows in Pennsylvania. Henceforth, the religious history of the Swedes followed the same eastward course that the pioneers themselves had taken.

Tollstadius' sudden death 3 years after the founding of the church failed to quiet the enthusiasm for religious home rule. The turbulent pastor was followed by the Rev. Jonas Aurén, the first definitely ordained minister of the Raccoon Church. Aurén's previous work among the English had made him fluent in their language. There must have been considerable English-speaking in the Swedish communities even by the time of his arrival in 1706, for he offered to conduct services in either Swedish or English. The parishioners, still close to the conservative ways of Björk and Rudman, firmly rejected the innovation. Aurén, however, probably spoke and taught a good deal of English during his 7-year term as minister at Raccoon.

Trinity Episcopal Church, Swedesboro, erected in 1784 near site of first Swedish Luthern Church in New Jersey. Became an Episcopal Church in 1786

THE RISE OF THE CHURCHES 77

The Raccoon Church, however, did not solve satisfactorily the problems of the Swedes in New Jersey. They had spread out so far between Pensauken Creek and the Maurice River that for many of them the new church was almost as difficult to reach as those across the river. It served mainly the colonists in the Repaupo, Raccoon and New Stockholm regions and the isolated settlements of the Helms, Dalbos and Rambos along the river front. Cinnaminson was too far north to be benefited, and Penns Neck too far south.

The sizable Penns Neck population was particularly affected. Determined to avoid the hardships of a journey either by water to Christina or overland to Raccoon, throughout Aurén's pastorship they agitated for a church of their own. The Penns Neck region at this time included the Swedes scattered along the river bank of Salem County and the Finns concentrated at Finns Point.

The Rev. Abraham Lidenius, who succeeded Aurén in 1713 at Raccoon, was sympathetic to their demands and helped them prepare a letter to Bishop Jesper Svedberg at Skara, asking permission to establish a parish in the region. Most of the Penns Neck people had continued, even after Raccoon Church was built, to attend Christina, and Pastor Björk there posted notices and called meetings, threatened and cajoled to halt the withdrawal of his parishioners. Lidenius was losing nothing by the construction of a new church. But Björk's income and the welfare of his parish were seriously threatened. These considerations weighed little upon the Penns Neck agitators; they were as determined as the Raccoon Swedes had been to have a church and a pastor of their own.

In the end they achieved complete independence from Christina but remained joined to Raccoon. Björk's term expired before the Swedish bishop had forwarded his authority for the Penns Neck parish, and he departed, admonishing his New Jersey members to remain within the fold. When the official sanction arrived, the Penns Neck group purchased land and began the construction of a church to be named for St. George.

It was dedicated in March 1717 by Dean Sandel. Lidenius was named pastor; in addition he was to continue his duties at Raccoon. With two churches of their own, both now approved by the Swedish Consistory, the New Jersey Swedes and Finns had broken the last religious bond with their countrymen across the Delaware.

Peace would have been welcome after a quarter of a century of ecclesiastical excitement. However, disputes and jealousies soon broke out among the New Jersey Swedes themselves. Pastor Lidenius was to serve each church on alternate Sundays, but both the Raccoon and Penns Neck parishes wanted him to live close at hand to officiate at baptisms, marriages and funerals. At first the common pastor "lived around" with members of both congregations, but with the growth of his family a parsonage became necessary. For several years the congregations battled with each other and with the harassed parson over the location of the proposed rectory and glebe. Finally, in 1720 a general compromise was effected by choosing land approximately midway between Raccoon and Penns Neck. The glebe became an integral part of the lives of both communities, for, with the exception of two years, the parishes always shared a common minister.

While the Swedes were victoriously bringing the Swedish Lutheran faith to the creeks of New Jersey, they were busy on another front which they considered equally important. It would profit them little to have a church and yet have their children educated in English or German schools. The first Swedish school had been set up in 1701 as a concession by Pastor Björk to the rebellious Raccoon colonists. Apparently the school disappeared when the parish broke with the church across the river. Five years later Pastor Aurén brought with him a young kinsman, Carl Brunjen, who had been a schoolmaster in Sweden. Brunjen established a school in Raccoon before the end of the year. Classes met in a small log building close by the church.

The Swedes had shown an interest in education almost from their arrival. A charter issued to Henry Hockhammen and Company in 1640 for the privilege of forming a settlement below Fort Christina stated: "The patrons of this colony shall be obliged to support at all times as many ministers and schoolmasters as the number of inhabitants shall seem to require." Shortly afterward John Campanius, following the European custom of uniting the functions of preacher and teacher, gave instructions at Printz's colony.

Perhaps the most famous school in New Sweden was that founded at Repaupo in 1715. Close as the region was to Raccoon, it was still isolated enough to feel that it required local instruction. The thoroughness with which it inculcated Swedish traditions and taught the Swedish language is obvious from the fact that two generations after its founding, Repaupo was the most Swedish of all the Swedish settlements in New Jersey.

Despite these two schools (and apparently there were no others), many, if not the majority, of the Swedish youth received their instruction in English schoolhouses, notably from Quaker teachers. Settlers in the Penns Neck region, those up Salem Creek and on Pensauken Creek soon heard their children reckoning sums in English, calculating time by the English calendar and chattering in the adopted tongue.

The rising rate of intermarriage, particularly with the English, in all probability helped to discourage and inhibit Swedish schools. The Nilssons of Raccoon married Eatons, the Locks at Penns Neck married Joneses, Brigitte Hoffman (Hopman) married Alexander King. Swedish couples frequently had English men and women stand as godparents for their children, a Cobb for a Didricsson infant, or a Pennington for an Anderson; sometimes they would ask a Dutchman, like Bilderback, to act as godfather for a Guilliamson. The fact that Swedes, Finns and Germans were all Lutherans of a sort facilitated these close relations. On the whole, church records of the Raccoon and Penns Neck congregations mount steadily through their early years with records of intermarriage, which in most cases must have meant a lessening of the Swedish bonds.

Church rituals, however, were carried on strictly in

Swedish, and when a lay preacher baptized Laurentz Cock's son, Thomas, at Salem in 1713, he specified in the church record that he had done so in English. Beyond the church and home, Anglicization was proceeding swiftly, but within these strongholds it was yet to encounter stern Swedish opposition.

XI

ENGLISH AND GERMAN INFLUENCES

THE two churches at Raccoon and Penns Neck continued throughout the eighteenth century to be the most important religious centers of the Swedes in New Jersey. Repositories of the slowly declining Swedish culture, they still had to struggle against inadequate support from the Consistory in Uppsala. In fact, at times the Consistory's behavior and attitude toward its charges in the New World bore an unfortunate resemblance to that of the New Sweden Company. And later events in the history of the churches carried the parallel even further.

Thus when Lidenius' successor, the Rev. Peter Tranberg, was transferred from Raccoon Church in 1741 after having served both Raccoon and Penns Neck for 15 years, the New Jersey Swedes were substantially back where they had started in their effort for church independence. The pulpits of the log buildings stood empty, the debts remained unpaid, and the Consistory made no move toward reviving the parishes with a new minister from Sweden.

Instead of humbly retracing their course across the river to the Gloria Dei or Christina churches, the Swedes resolved to do the best they could on their own soil. For a year they struggled with a lay teacher, but this effort was abandoned when the Penns Neck congregation failed to contribute its share toward his small income. Both churches were bitter about the withdrawal of Tranberg; the church record states in 1741: "For the people here . . . imagined Mr. Tranberg was now their bond-servant, since he had served them so long, and neither King nor Bishop of Sweden had anything to do with him, but they alone. And now when this Imagination failed them, some of them said with great indignation and malice that they wished never again to have anything to do with any Swedish minister."

This is the first record of outspoken opposition to the religious authority of the Swedish Crown and Consistory. The extremity of the statement suggests that the Swedes considered themselves forsaken in the American wilderness and would go elsewhere for their spiritual guidance. And this was exactly what they did.

Before it turned to other denominations, however, the Penns Neck congregation made a momentous decision. To the teacher's request for payment, members replied, "That since the congregation was now mostly English, they wished, after that day, to have their Services always in the English language, and entirely to give up their Swedish Church, to the Service of the English people, in order that the Congregation might be better enabled to support their teacher . . . It was then decided that after that day no Swedish Service should any more be held in the church of Penns Neck, but always English, with Prayers and Ceremonies according to the Church of England; which also is done."

The reasons for this were ample: first, financial, as stated by the members themselves; secondly, the Penns Neck section had been more English from the start than the other Swedish sections. Finally, the action offered a means of ending the interminable wrangles with the Raccoon Parish.

But the English victory was not yet complete. Instead of converting their simple house of worship into an Episcopal church, many of the Penns Neck parishioners joined with those at Raccoon in accepting religious leadership from the German Moravians.

Under the leadership of the Swedish-born Paul Daniel Bryzelius, Moravians had during the early 1740's opened a number of missions and prayer houses in South Jersey. Originally they had no intention of winning converts, but attempted only to supply religious services to places too poor to afford a minister. The Swedes undoubtedly qualified as needing their help, and by 1743 Moravians had begun to preach from the pulpits of Tollstadius and Lidenius. Bryzelius himself preached at Penns Neck and Raccoon. Some of the loyal members continued their Swedish Lutheranism under a lay reader, but many gratefully welcomed the services of the Moravians.

In joining with the Germans, the Delaware Valley Swedes and Finns were following a precedent which had been established by their countrymen in the hinterland. Those who pushed back into the land around the headwaters of Alloways Creek and the Cohansey River were followed by Germans who established a mission about 1690 for the scattered settlements loosely known as Cohansey. Justus Falckner, who set up the mission, was later (1703) ordained as a Lutheran minister by the Swedish pastors Björk, Sandel and Rudman. In 1726 the mission was converted into an Evangelical Lutheran Church, and was attended by both the Swedes and Germans in the region. The Rev. Peter Tranberg occasionally officiated in the pulpit until his transfer to Wilmington.

In 1739, shortly before Tranberg was transferred, the Swedish and German inlanders erected a log church building which has ever since been referred to as the Friesburg Church. The present building, which dates from 1768, is the only surviving church of Lutheran faith in the entire area once known as New Sweden.

The Friesburg Swedes had joined the Germans to obtain regular religious services, but had not sacrificed their Lutheranism. Another back country group, however, was obliged to follow the example of the Raccoon and Penns Neck Swedes and turn to the Moravian missionaries. In 1743 those Swedes who had pushed up the Maurice River Valley formed a congregation, but considered themselves affiliates of the Raccoon and Penns Neck parishes. At this time, however, there were no Swedish Lutheran ministers in New Jersey, and when their log church was erected in 1745, it was the Moravian Bryzelius who preached the first sermon. First known as the Maurice River Church, and later as the Port Elizabeth Church after that town came into existence, it continued for the next few years to be served by both Moravian missionaries and Swedish pastors.

The help offered by the Moravians increased the Swedes' religious problems instead of simplifying them. Conservatives of Raccoon and Penns Neck objected to the presence of the Germans in the Swedish pulpits and boycotted them. The colony was in danger of becoming rent once more by a severe religious dispute, when help finally came from Sweden. The Consistory liked the intrusion of the sectarian Moravians even less. It could not obtain the Swedish King's assent to eject them from the churches in America, but the local Swedes themselves accomplished this in 1745 by having the Gloucester County Court expel Bryzelius from the province on penalty of imprisonment.

Nevertheless, many Swedes joined neighboring congregations and intermarriages depleted the parishes even more. Alarmed by this drift away from the Swedish traditions and tongue, the Consistory in 1748 sent to Raccoon the Rev. Johan Sandin, with instructions to check the movement and revive the Swedish faith and language. Sandin was also appointed Dean of the Swedish Lutheran Churches in New Sweden. Thus, from having no minister at all, Raccoon was suddenly elevated to the position of being the center of Swedish religious activity in America. During Sandin's term of office all the churches in New Sweden were administered from New Jersey.

The Colony's ecclesiastical eminence was short-lived. Sandin died at Raccoon before he had been able to make much progress, and once more the New Jersey Swedes and Finns were without a minister. The breach was temporarily filled by Prof. Peter Kalm, friend of the dead pastor, a botanist who had been a theological student in his youth. Kalm had come to America in 1748 primarily to study plant life and other scientific subjects for his university at Åbo (Turku), Finland, but he willingly conducted lay services at Raccoon, his headquarters.

Matters improved in 1749 when the Rev. Eric Unander arrived at Raccoon as the assistant of the Rev. Israel Acrelius, who was to be pastor there and Dean in the Province. Shortly before Acrelius sailed, the sudden death of Tranberg again crippled the Consistory's plans for building a strong New Jersey branch of the church. The Consistory then sent Acrelius to Christina as pastor and made Unander full pastor of Raccoon and Penns Neck parishes.

Site of the Maurice River Church, Founded in 1743 near Port Elizabeth

Nothnagle House near Repaupo, showing original Swedish log cabin

The arrival of Acrelius in 1750 was almost melodramatic in its timeliness. And with equal drama the man fitted the job which had been created from a decade of drift, disregard and disunion. Next to Printz and Nicholas Collin, a later Raccoon minister, Israel Acrelius was probably the most capable and colorful figure in the entire history of the Swedes of New Jersey. His career was marked by a keen personal enthusiasm for the New World and a restless desire to know its history and its people. He learned so much and so well that in 1759 he published *A History of New Sweden; or, the Settlements on the River Delaware,* still one of the best histories of New Sweden. The first had been written in 1702 by Thomas Campanius Holm, grandson of Printz's preacher.

The demand for English services and sermons in the Swedish churches had become loud among the young people of the communities at the time Acrelius took up his duties. The long absence of inspiration from Sweden had quickened the process of assimilation, and many Swedes were definitely ranged against the old order. Kalm, in fact, had found Repaupo in 1749 the only place where Swedish was still spoken "in its purest form . . . without one word of English being mixed in." Repaupo, which had been declining in importance for years in favor of Raccoon, cut off from the main highway across which passed the new and sophisticated currents, was a natural Swedish stronghold. But Kalm found there only 70 inhabitants.

Surveying the entire region, Acrelius reported that there were barely 200 persons still able to speak Swedish. His concern mounted to anxiety when he noticed in the church registers and record books the frequent mixture of English, German and Latin with the proper Swedish. Since 1742, of course, the Penns Neck congregation had been having lay services performed in English, but there had been no Swedish minister using the adopted tongue.

Acrelius was willing to make some concessions to the changes of the day. He advised henceforth that records be kept in the Latin script instead of the traditional Swedish, "In order that those of our People who understand

Swedish and Write English may thus be able to read the Church Records, since no Swedish-American[1] understands the Swedish style of writing any longer."

On the preservation of the language, however, he was firm. "The Swedish language, in America, now on its last leg, may be saved," he predicted. Acrelius was as good as his word. If, during his term as Dean, Swedish did not again become the common language of the colonists, it at least regained some of its ecclesiastical position. The church records between 1750 and 1756 are considerably purer than those before, and sermons and rituals were carried on according to the Dean's wish.

Acrelius was fortunate in having two ardent assistants in his revival work in New Jersey. Pastor Unander warmly supported the return to the old ways, and in a short time the Raccoon parish had grown enough to require a curate. To this office was appointed the Rev. Johan Abraham Lidenius, son of the third pastor of the congregations, and the first Swedish Lutheran minister born in America. In addition to helping Unander at Raccoon and Penns Neck, young Lidenius assisted him in his periodic visits to the outlying Maurice River Church and the Friesburg Church as well. In the barren years before the coming of the energetic Acrelius and his staff, German ministers had been even more successful in establishing themselves in the inland pulpits and wilderness preaching stations established by the Swedes. There had even been an Englishman, one John Wade, out at Maurice River Church during 1748-49.

The infiltration of English into Raccoon and Penns Neck had been too great, however, for Acrelius. He made further concessions and permitted Unander to indulge in what he called "double preaching, first in Swedish, then in English." He also allowed the New Jersey pastor to "distribute his labor to the English congregation in Salem, as also to the people upon Timber Creek, though only on week-days." It is doubtful whether Acrelius is here referring to Englishmen, or to Swedes whose habits already made them as an "English congregation." Certainly there

---

1. Possibly this was the first use of the term "Swedish-American."

had been many Swedes in and around Salem and on the estates of Timber Creek.

Acrelius himself gives a vivid picture of the incessant struggle for the preservation of the native tongue:

Sometimes it is concluded in the Vestry that no more English preaching shall be held, no English any more be buried in the grave-yard. Then the Minister and his Church officers are decried as persons who regard all English as heathens . . . So this must be changed again.

One will have his child baptized in English, another in Swedish, at one and the same hour in the Church. Some refuse to stand as Sponsors if the child is not baptized in Swedish, and yet it may be that the other Sponsors do not understand it . . . When funeral sermons are preached, English people of every form of faith come together, and then it often happens that the one desires preaching in English, the other in Swedish, and that just as the Minister is going into the Church.

On the extent and reasons for the growth of English, Acrelius was even more to the point:

It is here necessary to state how far these Swedish churches are inclined to have their service in English. The Swedes formerly dwelt more closely together, used their language more among themselves and daily at home in their houses; when it happens that the old among our people do not speak English well, can hardly read an English book or clearly understand English preaching; and, in a word they hate in their hearts everything that is English. They say that they are Swedish people, although they are in an English country.

Some of the young people have learnt both languages, and bring up their children in the same manner, as they speak Swedish in their houses, and let the children take their chance of learning English outside the house . . . All those who understand and speak and read Swedish are entirely in favor of Divine service in their own language. Others, again, whose wives, children, relatives and friends are English, cannot but desire worship for them in that language which they understand, especially as they, upon their side, contribute to support the Minister and church, are descendants of Swedes, and do not wish to fall away from their church, and have also many members of the English church among them, who in like manner need Divine Service, and will help to support the Minister.

Written in 1759 or before, these statements accurately foreshadow the outcome of the language conflict. The old grew fewer and the young more numerous.

XII

A PORTRAIT OF NEW SWEDEN

THE Swedish culture was losing out on other fronts besides that of language. By the decade 1750-60 the Swedes had all but fused into the community life of the English. The old folkways lingered on in such isolated inland regions as Repaupo, or with the oldest members of the settlements on the creeks. For the most part, however, observers from Sweden at this period found the growing Americanism of the colony more interesting than the dying *Svenskheten i allmänhet* (i. e. the Swedish ways in general).

The three great descriptive records of the Swedes of New Jersey, Peter Kalm's *Travels*, Israel Acrelius' *History* and Nicholas Collin's *Journal*, were written by men sensitive to the essential qualities of the Old and New World. Kalm and Acrelius deal chiefly with the years around 1750, while Collin picks up the story in 1770. Jointly the three books mark the inevitable march of the Swedes of New Jersey toward Americanism. And when each author's particular emphasis is scraped away, there remains a clear, running picturization of the Swedes as they lived, worked and took their place in Colonial society; vivid, authentic vignettes of the average Swedes of New Jersey.

It must be remembered that the Swedes of New Jersey had in the main emigrated from the west bank of the Delaware, and that some time after communities had been established the New Jersey colonists were still pioneering. Therefore, many of the customs and methods of solving frontier problems which had been developed by the original Swedes from abroad were reused after the second immigration of the New Jersey Swedes. No matter what they had brought with them from the west bank, when they settled on the creeks flowing into the Delaware they faced the basic problem of all colonists: food, shelter and clothing.

Title page of the Raccoon and Penns Neck Church Register

Pages from the Raccoon and Penns Neck Church Register (Swedish Text)

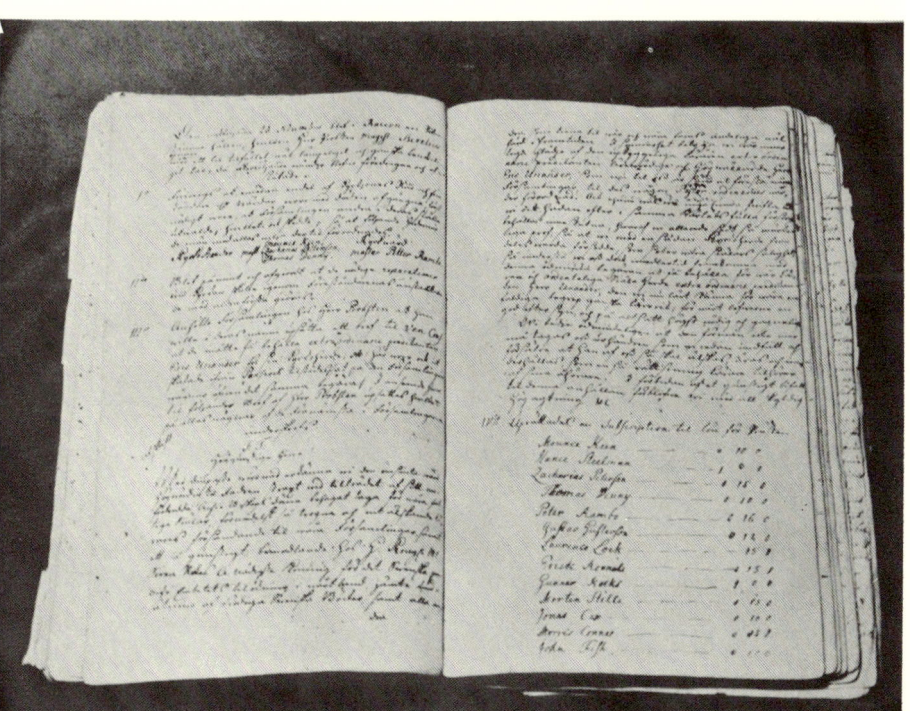

Originally, then, the Swedes and Finns of New Jersey doubtless built the same kinds of log cabins which had been erected at Christina, Tinicum and Fort Elfsborg. Experienced woodsmen, the Swedes have been credited with introducing the log cabin to America, for such were the homes of many who dwelt in the vast Swedish forest lands. Some of the Finnish dwellings were shaped like a cone and resembled Indian tepees; others were rounded like Eskimos' igloos. But no matter what the shape, all the wooden structures showed the general Swedish characteristic of joining logs by notching. Beds in the log cabins were built bunklike along the walls. The space between the beds was used for a linen closet under which chickens and ducks were kept in the winter.

The first churches were of similar log construction, and it was apparently not until the arrival of the English that the Swedes exchanged rude cabins for brick houses, holes in the logs for glass windows, and clay for plaster. By 1700, however, they were building in South Jersey the tall, narrow brick houses which have come to be known as "Swedish Colonial style." Nevertheless, many of the less wealthy Swedes continued to build frame and even log houses. Similarly, in the rich homes there was considerable furniture of delicate and expensive design, while the poorer dwellings were furnished with the rude slabs, stools and pallets of the earlier days. Local woods were widely used; sometimes purposefully, as in the case of sassafras, which Kalm noted was used to expel bedbugs by its scent. The houses were illumined by fragrant native bayberry candles.

The colonists dropped their native costume soon after they arrived and never donned it again. At first, scarcity of cloth made skins and furs obligatory; later the colonists followed the English style. The men wore the typical Colonial suit of wool stuffs, and the women made their dresses from calico and cotton. Linen was especially sought after because of the oppressive lowland heat. Since there were few Swedes in the larger towns of West Jersey, most of their clothing was doubtless homemade.

Acrelius describes elaborate meals and considerable variety in meats on some Swedish tables, but his account of country fare is probably more typical of the diet of the New Jersey Swedes: "for breakfast, in summer, cold milk and bread, rice, milk-pudding, cheese and butter, cold meat. In winter, mush and milk, and milk porridge, hominy and milk. The same also serves for supper, if so desired." The noon meal was even heavier, consisting of "soup, fresh meat, dried beef, and bacon, with cabbage, apples, potatoes, Turkish beans, large beans, all kinds of roots, mashed turnips, pumpkins, several kinds of fruits and a couple of pies."

Fish, a staple in Sweden, was eaten sparingly in the New World, and only when dried and salted. Tea, coffee and chocolate were used everywhere. Kalm found the people of Repaupo making tea from the chips and shavings of white cedar, which they assured him "they preferred in regard to its wholesomeness to all foreign tea." He found few Swedish dishes on the tables of the Swedes; even *knäckebröd* (cracker-hole-bread) was baked only by the clergymen from Sweden. Of spirits there was an abundance: Acrelius lists 44 different alcoholic beverages in use around 1750, but it is generally thought that the Swedes consumed mostly beer and homemade wine.

Oysters, found in abundance off the South Jersey shore, were exceedingly popular with the Swedes. Kalm records the old adage that "oysters are best in those months which have 'r' in their names, as September, October, etc., but they are not so good in other months." He adds that, then as now, there were poor people who lived all year long upon practically nothing but oysters and a little bread.

During his travels in the Delaware Valley, Kalm noted the absence of Swedish turnips, although the area contained many first generation Swedes as well as descendants of pioneers. Regretfully he wrote, "Nobody around here had ever heard of rutabagas or Swedish turnips." Dr. Nicholas Collin determined to do something about this favorite Swedish dish after he arrived in 1770. In the course of importing and exporting seeds and plants between America and Sweden, he received Swedish turnip seeds, and Dr. Amandus Johnson believes, " . . . it is likely that it was Collin who introduced the rutabaga to this country."

Agriculture and grazing were the major economic activities of the colonists. Corn, rye, wheat, oats and potatoes appear to have been the most common products. At first, the Swedes continued the cooperative type of farming, sharing implements and labor, that they had known in Sweden; later, however, farming became an individual matter, and large landowners leased sections of their property to tenants. Horses, cattle and sheep were the chief stock owned by the Swedes. Acrelius thought the wool from the Swedish sheep superior to that of the English. The hogs of the Swedes had so multiplied by Kalm's time that they ran wild in the woods, and people shot them as needed.

Because they had no fences, the Swedish colonists identified their hogs by ear marks. A 1686 document, recently brought to light by Frank H. Stewart, Gloucester County historian, reveals the character and variety of these markings. Most of them were made by slitting or cropping the hog's ear, sometimes in a particular design. Usually both ears were marked, each differently. For example, the hogs of John Hopman of Raccoon bore a swallowtail with a half moon on the underside on the right ear, and a plain swallowtail on the left. Andreas Anderson from Stockholm Township marked his hogs by leaving the left ear whole, except for a hole plunged in the middle, and cropping and piercing the right ear. At Mantua Creek, Peter Dalbo kept the left ear whole and simply placed a swallowtail on the right one.

The Swedes also had their agricultural difficulties. Peas could not be planted because of insects which devoured them; pasture lands were poor compared to those in Sweden; fruit trees were almost annually ruined by caterpillars. Kalm must have been among the earliest to realize how the Colonial farmers were misusing the soil. In a remarkably modern passage he observes that the Swedes sowed uncultivated grounds as long as they would produce a crop without manuring, only to turn them into pastures when they would produce no more; then they would seek new spots. Kalm saw this as dangerous for the fields, meadows, cattle and forests, and lamented that "the characteristics of the English nation, so well skilled in husbandry, is scarcely recognizable here."

Land was cheap and plentiful; taxes were low; and apparently the Swedes kept moving from one tract to another along the creek they had chosen. Kalm encountered little poverty in his travels among the thrifty and frugal Swedes and commented that the liberties men enjoyed were so great that a man "considers himself a prince in his possessions." By banking swamp land along the river with dikes, the Swedes created additional arable land which proved especially suitable for raising grain. These dikes also provided water power for various kinds of mills.

Large families were facilitated by the abundance of land, and visitors from Sweden were frequently impressed by the size of American families compared to those in Sweden. Baptism records indicate that 10 or 12 children was more likely the rule than the exception. Måns Keen of Raccoon could count 45 living children, grandchildren and great-grandchildren, which caused Kalm to observe that "he had been uncommonly blessed."

Disease, however, was a real threat to the population of New Sweden. Epidemics of pricks and smallpox from time to time carried off large sections of the population. Indians often caught the smallpox from the Swedes and died in great numbers. Snakes were a constant menace, and ague, or malarial fever, was a common ailing. The remedies used by the Swedes for ague reveal a curious mixture of science, Indian lore and medieval alchemy. A popular one was a mixture of Jesuit bark, the bark of the root of the tulip tree and the dogwood, powdered sulphur mixed with sugar, yellow bark of the peach tree, and the leaves of the *Potentilla reptans*. These were brewed in some form of a tea. Others ranged from a baked apple stuffed with spider's web to a mixture of lemon juice and sage.

Kalm was much interested in his discovery that the

Europeans in North America lost their teeth much sooner than in Europe. Scientifically, he went through a large number of possible causes, including change of air, weather, greater consumption of fruit and sweets, and finally hit upon tea as the likely solution. He observed that both Indian and European women who drank large quantities of tea lost their teeth prematurely, while those who had not used tea retained their teeth to old age. His theory, however, was rudely upset when he learned from several young women that they had lost their teeth before they had begun to drink tea. Without refuting this fact, he finally decided somewhat lamely that the early loss of teeth was due to the women's habit of drinking tea before they let it cool, concluding that the extreme heat damaged their teeth.

The Swedes used the native tobacco plant as a remedy for several afflictions. They tied the leaves around their feet and arms when they had ague and prepared a tea from the leaves for dysentery. They also made a concoction from the leaves which they injected into cattle suffering from worms. It was reputed to kill the worms and make them fall out of the animal's body.

Wherever he went, Kalm observed in the reminiscences of the older people the steady growth of English customs among the Swedes. Old Nils Gustafson of Raccoon, for example, told him that until the English arrived the Swedes used to bathe regularly every Saturday in separate bathhouses, similar to those found in Sweden, but that now the bathhouses had been done away with. Kalm gives no hint as to whether this meant increased or decreased ablution. In the old man's boyhood Swedes had made knives, hatchets and scythes in the Swedish style, but they now imitated the English. Even more significant was his lament that not even Christmas was celebrated with the traditional Swedish games and dishes, as it once had been.

Of customs that might be considered original with the Swedes of New Jersey, Kalm and Acrelius found little trace. Kalm noted an amusing marriage custom, which may, however, have been English in its sources. A widow left in poverty by her husband had to be remarried in her nightgown. This odd bridal raiment was chosen to indicate to her dead husband's creditors that she left them all her clothes and everything they could find in the house. Then she was not obliged to pay them anything further, because she had given them everything she owned, save the nightgown, which law permitted her to keep. Modest bridegrooms sometimes circumvented this custom by lending—not giving—new clothes to their prospective brides.

The general picture that the informal and formal historians give of the Swedes of New Jersey is that of an industrious people, steadily adopting more and more New World ways, with a strong, lingering feeling for their old-time religion. As in the rest of Colonial America, the Bible was the most widely read and widely quoted book among the Swedish colonists. Save for a reference by Collin to horse racing at Raccoon, little is known of their amusements, but it is extremely likely that they depended in large part upon the church for their social as well as spiritual life. It must be remembered that the drift toward English in the church service indicated no loosening in the church cords drawn about the Swedish communities.

Pastors from Tollstadius on were the dominant figures in the Swedish settlements. The parishioners might underpay their ministers and fail to provide them with adequate living conditions, but they respected their word as law. The divines served not only as the spiritual leaders but also as judges of family disputes, teachers, amateur or first-aid doctors, family counselors and advisers on everything from crops to politics. In fact, there is reason to believe that from time to time these Swedish pastors involved themselves too freely in local politics and business. When Acrelius arrived in 1750 as Dean, he admonished his fellow clergymen to desist from further interference in purely secular affairs.

Despite such breaches, the pastor and his church remained the heart of New Sweden in New Jersey. The deeply religious Swedes, capable of considerable heat and dispute over their religious problems and difficulties, were

Silver Communion Set purchased by the Raccoon Parish more than two hundred years ago and still in use

equally capable of going to extreme lengths to guarantee themselves the continuance of religious worship. This expression of the religious spirit is perhaps the dominant note in the history of the Swedes and Finns of New Jersey, and oddly enough, to a great extent, the cause for the extinction of the early Swedish Evangelical Lutheran Church.

XIII

THE SECOND FALL OF NEW SWEDEN

THE Rev. Israel Acrelius returned to Sweden in 1756. He left the New Jersey Swedish churches considerably strengthened in morals and numbers. In the year of his departure Johan Abraham Lidenius succeeded Pastor Unander at the Raccoon and Penns Neck parishes, and the young man's skill and industry promised continued improvement for the Swedish Lutheran cause in New Jersey.

Lidenius was a popular preacher who traveled extensively around the colony, and even as far west as Reading, Pa. He remained pastor for 6 years which seem to have been among the most peaceful in the history of the joint congregations. In 1762 Lidenius was succeeded by the Rev. Johan Wicksell, whose extreme conservatism ignited anew the flame of discontent with the maintenance of the Swedish traditions. Oddly enough, as the demand for English mounted in 1763, the town of Raccoon was renamed Swedesboro.

Only two years after Wicksell had assumed his duties, the preference for English had grown so strong that the Swedesboro and Penns Neck parishes decided henceforth to keep their church records in English, so that they might be understood by the entire congregation. Nevertheless, the records of the remainder of his pastorship are extremely scanty; in fact, beyond births, deaths and marriages there are no entries at all for some years. Matters grew worse in 1765 when the church was granted a charter by the English Crown, in the face of its traditional spiritual allegiance to the King of Sweden.

The Consistory, whose authority in the Colony was rapidly becoming almost negligible, made another attempt to save its churches. In 1768 Wicksell was made Vice Dean of the Delaware River parishes. His assistant at Swedesboro and Penns Neck was to be a brilliant 24-year-old minister, Nicholas Collin. He arrived in America in 1770, bringing with him Wicksell's commission, which, in the absence of a Dean, placed him in charge of the Swedish churches on the river. For the next 3 years Swedesboro again became the center of Swedish religious activity in the country.

Wicksell's new duties obliged him to be absent frequently from his pulpits, and Collin virtually assumed the position of rector from the time of his arrival. He had sojourned in England for several months before embarking for America and added English to a long list of languages he already knew. His linguistic accomplishments met with instantaneous favor in both congregations, especially Penns Neck, which from the outset had been more English than Swedesboro.

In his *Journal* Collin has left an interesting account of his diligence in preparing himself to deliver sermons in English: "After a short time I could easily preach in English without copy, though of course the pronunciation of certain words was necessarily faulty. During the entire first year I used to spend three to four hours a day reading the best English sermons, moral and historic authors and some poets. Through this method one quickly gains proficiency in the language and collects a good understanding of various subjects, and need not copy portions from others, which really will not fit in with what one had written oneself. Pronunciation is more easily learned from poetry by the similar rhyme endings in words which are differently written."

The young minister traveled around the Colony and preached several times at the Maurice River Church, which had been struggling along with whatever leadership, Swedish, German or Dutch, had come its way. He also spoke at preaching stations between Swedesboro and Penns Neck and ministered to various English Protestant sects scattered around the colony.

On the state of Swedish at the time of his arrival, Collin observed that "all those who partly speak and understand the language number about 200 persons." This was the same estimate made by Acrelius 20 years before. Collin also noted that no more than 80 or 90 persons attended Swedish services, that the Penns Neck congregation was entirely English, and that the Swedish congregation in Swedesboro was far outnumbered by the English.

By 1774 the attitude of the people of South Jersey had become so anti-British that, probably from their fear of seditious utterances, British officials hampered all services except those in English churches. For 4 years, from 1774 to 1778, worship at Swedesboro and Penns Neck was conducted only at rare intervals. Many Swedes turned once more to the English denominations for regular services.

The majority of the Swedes and Finns in the region emphatically sided with the Revolutionists. During the early years of the war the contending armies marched and countermarched along Kings Highway, with much of their activity centered at Swedesboro. The church was used at different times to billet both American and British troops, and Collin on more than one occasion was crowded to the wall in his parsonage by British officers. On the muster rolls of the Colonial forces of Gloucester and Salem Counties appear a number of Swedish and Finnish names, many of them family names of the late seventeenth century pioneers in New Jersey. Among the captains from Upper Penns Neck were John Helms and William Dalbow, and in the cavalry were David Hendrickson and John Heuling. From Salem County came representatives of the old Rambo and Lock families as well as Capt. Andrew Sinnickson. On the other hand, Collin reports some sentiment for the British, particularly among merchants who resented the Continental Congress' decree forbidding trade with the enemy army. The entire region welcomed the shift of the war northward.

In 1778 Collin succeeded Wicksell as pastor, in title as well as fact. He immediately began to plan for a new church. The old one, erected more than 70 years before by Tollstadius, had been in poor condition when Collin arrived and the quartering of soldiers had further weakened it. It had escaped the torch in the British attacks on the town but was no longer safe for worship.

THE SECOND FALL OF NEW SWEDEN 99

The pastor pushed subscriptions vigorously. Despite the fact that the town had been hard hit by incessant British requisitions for grain, cattle, and even silverware, Collin's appeal for building funds resulted in the subscription of £1,418, of which £1,310 was collected. With this the erection of the new church was undertaken. The untiring pastor himself inspected all bricks, lumber, stone and other materials and added his own labor to that of the bricklayers and other mechanics. The church was designed for future expansion of the congregation, and Collin worked on the project as though it were opening a new day in the history of the Swedish church in America.

Actually the erection of the present church at Swedesboro all but closed the story of the Swedes and their church in New Jersey. Prophetically the altar and pulpit were engraved in the American style, and the exterior resembled the Georgian Colonial design of the English. The unfinished building was dedicated in 1784, but Collin continued to solicit funds from the congregations for its completion.

Two years after the dedication, with the church still lacking paneling and whitewashing, the building was transferred to the Episcopal Church in America. Its name was changed from the Swedish Evangelical Lutheran Church at Swedesboro to Trinity Episcopal Church, as it is known today. Collin was asked to remain until an ordained Episcopal rector could be obtained.

The long controversy with Sweden and the Swedish Consistory was over. The Swedes had by this time become not only English, but American as well. Religious bonds with the Old World were severed along with political ties. The incident which caused the inevitable break with the Consistory was a royal decree providing that the Swedesboro and Penns Neck congregations would have to defray the travel expenses of future ministers, both coming and returning to Sweden, as well as guaranteeing them decent support. The Consistory showed that it realized the weak state of the church in New Jersey by ruling that future ministers who served there would no longer be entitled to superior privileges and preferments. It further commented on the virtual death of the Swedish tongue which was characterized as "the principal tie of their connection with Sweden."

According to Collin, the joint congregations, laboring under the expense of a new church and still "feeling the disaster of a calamitous war," were reluctant to undertake any additional expense. With sermons already being preached mostly in English and the Swedish-speaking population dying off, there seemed no advantage in further union with the Consistory. Accordingly they turned themselves over to the Episcopal Church. Collin departed from New Jersey early in 1786, and with him went the last vestige of the Consistory's authority.

The Rev. Jehu C. Clay, a nineteenth century pastor at Gloria Dei Church, has explained why the Swedes, who for generations had close relations with the German Lutherans, chose instead the Episcopal Church. While there was no dissimilarity in doctrine between the Swedish Lutheran and German Lutheran churches, they were entirely different in administration. The Swedish Church, although Lutheran in doctrine, was episcopal in government. With a hierarchy and apostolic succession like that of the Consistory, the Episcopal administration appealed more to the Swedes than the similarities of faith in German Lutheranism. It was also likely that the more English or American characteristics of the Episcopal Church strongly influenced their choice.

Nicholas Collin (1748-1831), last Swedish Lutheran minister of New Jersey churches, at the death of Benjamin Franklin

XIV

THE SWEDES AND FINNS AS AMERICANS

THE passing of the Swedish Evangelical Lutheran Church at Swedesboro marked the eclipse of Swedish culture in New Jersey. Like the other nationalities which had originally come to found colonies and remained to build a new nation, the Swedes, already highly integrated with the English, easily became Americans. A new country with limitless pioneering possibilities and a new century crowded with invention and change afforded a poor soil for the preservation of Old World ways. Almost from the date of the founding of the Republic, records of the New Jersey Swedes as Swedes cease. The Swedish culture began a long slumber from which it was not to stir for almost a century.

The process which had begun as early as 1700 speeded toward completion throughout the nineteenth century. The few remaining old people who could speak Swedish died, and with them perished the use of the language in daily life. Intermarriage with the English, Dutch, Germans and Scotch-Irish became even more prevalent and wiped out traces of Swedish living in the homes. Swedes and Finns who had fought vigorously for an independent America caught admirably the new spirit of Americanism and were quick to shed the vestiges of their Europeanism. The collapse of Swedish churches and their replacement by English Protestant houses of worship cut completely any religious bond with Sweden.

Similarly the rise of publicly supported schools continued the work of the English schools of the previous century. Young Swedes learned solely the language and thought of the new country, for there was none to teach the old ways. Only the funeral of an aged Swede, the accidental discovery of a Colonial record or some sentimental momento recalled the days of the Swedish pastors and loyalty to the Swedish Crown.

Sweden itself, however, had not lost interest in America. There had been an active trade with the Colonies during the Revolutionary War in tar, pitch, steel and iron, and with the establishment of peace, Sweden decided to negotiate a treaty of commerce and friendship with the new state. As an investigator of political and economic conditions in the United States King Gustavus III selected Samuel Gustaf Hermelin. Ostensibly he was only to travel in America on a scientific mission, like Peter Kalm before him. In 1783 Hermelin inspected the iron-producing areas throughout the east, including many in New Jersey, and returned to Sweden to write his *Report about the Mines in the United States of America*. The treatise is still considered of great value by mining authorities. Hermelin, incidentally, had come to this country with a commission naming him the Swedish Minister to the United States, but he did not become the first Swedish diplomatic representative, because the United States failed to appoint a Minister to Sweden.

The Swedes continued to move about South Jersey in the early years of the nineteenth century, following in the paths blazed a hundred years before by Eric Mullica and James Steelman. Petersons, Ericksons and Hoffmans were among the original settlers of Leesburg in Cumberland County, founded by two Englishmen. Swedes also accompanied another Englishman, Peter Reeve, to nearby Dorchester, which was likewise founded shortly after 1800.

Throughout the succeeding quarter of a century they kept moving across the State in small numbers to settlements along Delaware Bay, notably to Port Norris at the mouth of the Maurice River, and farther east into Cape May County, where Swedes are believed to have settled originally in the late years of the seventeenth century. These Delaware Bay settlers forsook the traditional agriculture of their countrymen and plunged into the oyster and fish industries, ultimately finding their way back to the ancient Swedish occupations of commercial navigation and shipbuilding.

Throughout the first third of the nineteenth century

the Swedes in the Raccoon and Penns Neck region maintained a slender relationship with old Sweden through the person of their former pastor, Nicholas Collin. He had quickly become a notable figure in Philadelphia, the friend of Washington, Jefferson, Franklin and other leaders of the new Nation. Although probably not in his official capacity, the clergyman was present at the death of Benjamin Franklin in Philadelphia in 1790.

Established as he was at Gloria Dei Church, Collin had made too many friends across the river to isolate himself from the region. While his former parishioners became devout Episcopalians, the old Lutheran pastor journeyed up the creeks to visit the scenes of what had once been a flourishing Swedish section. With his death in 1831, however, this tie was broken. Thereafter, New Jersey Swedes interested in Sweden or Swedish ways had to depend upon infrequent visits to or visitors from the mother country.

In 1834 the first history of the Province of New Sweden, by Thomas Campanius Holm, was translated into English. There must have been a revival of interest in the colony then, for the following year Jehu Curtis Clay, successor at Gloria Dei to Collin, published his *Annals of the Swedes on the Delaware*. At that time, however, there was not a Swedish Lutheran Church in the Delaware Valley.

The Swedes who lived in New Jersey along the creeks first settled by their ancestors continued to follow their agricultural way of life. They contributed to the development of the section as it grew into one of the great tomato and dairy farming tracts in the United States. Old newspaper files occasionally recount the activities of a Swede descended from the original settlers of the region. A member of the Rambo family, pillars of Tollstadius' Swedish Lutheran church, is reported in 1853 as an Episcopal missionary. And a union of two old Swedish names occurs in that of Helmes Vanneman, a Swedesboro businessman of the same period. There are similar echoes in the firm of Lock, Lock and Fisher at Repaupo.

For the most part, however, public records of the pre-Civil War period are barren of Swedish names. The Swedes, for one thing, had no tradition of officeholding, for as early as 1702 the British had shut the small Swedish landholders out of the competition by requiring the ownership of 1,000 acres of land as a qualification for membership in the assembly. With the exception of a local official here and there, mayors and sheriffs, the Swedes of South Jersey seem to have taken little part in the administration of either their counties or their State.

By the middle of the century Swedes had moved north along the Atlantic Coast as far as Barnegat on the island of Long Beach. History tended to repeat itself here, for the Swedes mingled with the Dutch in a community devoted almost exclusively to seafaring life. The old names of Erickson and Anderson recur in Barnegat records alongside Dutch names such as Falkinburg and Inman. This community rapidly became dominated by Swedes, one of the few towns in New Jersey which succeeded in attracting emigrants from Sweden. Possibly this resulted from the maritime life of the community.

Although Swedish immigration to the United States had been rising since 1850, disastrous crop failures in Sweden in 1867-69 significantly increased the number of immigrants. During the next decade Swedish arrivals averaged 15,000 a year, and the number rose steadily until it reached an all-time high of 39,000 in 1903. This immigration was part of a general European movement to the promised land of America. Swedes, however, often had special motives. The development of the agricultural lands in the American middle west seriously affected farming in their homeland. Some came to this country because of religious or social discrimination, while others fled to escape compulsory military service. In the 1890's and early 1900's the growth of factories in Sweden resulted in labor conflicts and economic crises which prompted many Swedes to seek a new start in a new country.

Only a small proportion of these Swedes came to New Jersey. And most of these immigrants continued to be attracted to the metropolitan area rather than to southern New Jersey. Occasionally, however, new arrivals from

Crown Prince Gustaf Adolf of Sweden, Official Representative to the
Tercentenary Celebration

Sweden did seek the soil settled by the Colonial Swedes. In 1874 several families from Sweden purchased land near Franklinville in Gloucester County, and a few years before a settlement of Swedish farmers existed in the vicinity of Malaga. It is thought that one of these Malaga citizens, Jassen Skaarup, helped develop the Franklinville settlement.

The year 1874 marks a turning point in Swedish consciousness in the East, for it was then that Israel Acrelius' *History of New Sweden* was first translated into English and published in the United States. The centennial of American Independence, celebrated two years later, helped to awaken interest in all phases of American history and served to make Swedish-Americans sensitive to their nation's part in the development of America. As historical and genealogical societies became more important, gradually more and more information was revealed about the half-forgotten role of Sweden in the New World. For the Swedes of New Jersey, however, there was a decided drawback; most of the research and publication dealt with the settlements on the west bank of the Delaware River, those made while Sweden remained in control of her Colony. The story of the New Jersey churches and the Swedish penetration of the Jersey interior remained for the most part untold.

Interest in the history of New Sweden reached a climax in 1909 with the founding of the Swedish Colonial Society at Philadelphia. On its rolls were immediately found the names of many Swedish families which recalled the original voyages up the creeks of New Jersey. Among these were the Sinnicksons of Salem and the Rambos of Gloucester County. Two years later the first scholarly treatise on the history of New Sweden, *The Swedish Settlements on the Delaware*, was published by Dr. Amandus Johnson. In 1915 popular interest warranted the revision of this work in a one-volume edition.

Constant intermarriage gradually obliterated the physical characteristics of the Swedes and Finns, and by the twentieth century they were virtually indistinguishable from the other nationalities in South Jersey. The Anglicization of names had continued, although often the Swedish origin was apparent. For example, Bengston changed to Banks, Kyn to Keen, Bonde to Boon, Svenson to Swanson, Whiler to Wheeler, Hopman to Hoffman, and Jonesson to Jones. Given names were similarly altered, Per to Peter, Lars to Lawrence, Nils to Nicholas, and Olave to William.

Place names in southern New Jersey, however, retained a strong Swedish cast. The old New Stockholm Township now includes the three towns of Bridgeport, Gibbstown and Nortonville; Finnstown has changed to Finns Point, but there survive Repaupo, Rambo Station, Dalbo's Landing, Helm's Cove, Elsinborough Township, and Swedesboro itself. As noted earlier, Eric Mullica and James Steelman left their names over a wide area of the coastal region. A few Swedish names are even of comparatively recent origin, as in the case of New Sweden Crossroad in Gloucester County and Swedes Run in both Burlington and Salem Counties.

Yet in the southern part of the State persons of Swedish descent are no longer concentrated in the historically Swedish regions. Gloucester and Salem Counties were the eighteenth century strongholds of the Swedes. According to the 1930 census, these two counties contain only one-seventh of the Swedes in southern New Jersey. Atlantic and Cape May Counties, once sparsely settled with Swedes, now have more than one-third of the South Jersey total.

Present-day Swedes in the southern part of the State are either descendants of pioneer families or comparatively recent arrivals. The former have generally followed their ancestors' agricultural tradition, although many have entered trade and the professions. The native-born and first-generation Swedes, however, have gone back to the maritime life. The fishing industry of the region, both deep sea and oyster, is practically dominated by Swedes.

Angelsea, near Wildwood in Cape May County, is the headquarters for large fishing fleets. They are operated by six companies, the largest of which is headed by Sven

SWEDES AND FINNS AS AMERICANS 107

Marthin, a native-born son of Swedish parentage. Latest available figures show that at least 500 Swedes are engaged in fishing at or near Wildwood. Many of them agree with Mr. Marthin's reason for coming to Wildwood and its environs, when he asserted, "The first Swedes came to the Delaware just as the Germans came to Pennsylvania, and they still come here."

Other Swedes of the region have gone into another ancient Swedish industry, shipbuilding. The shipyards of South Jersey, particularly the large plants in Camden, employ many Swedes as mechanics and engineers, while the smaller boat-building yards in the extreme southern part of the State also depend upon traditional Swedish skill in this industry.

The Swedish church in Angelsea is the focal point for the observance of Swedish national customs and traditions in the Cape May, Cumberland and Atlantic County region. Another center is the Wildwood Chapter of the Vasa Order of America, a national fraternity of Swedish-Americans, which numbers here 250 members. There are also chapters in Atlantic City and Camden.

The descendants of the Swedes of Colonial times are still concentrated in Camden, Gloucester and Salem Counties. Town and city directories in these sections are studded with names transplanted from abroad while New Sweden was still a political entity in the Delaware Valley. Among them are Hanson, Tallman, Mecum, Steelman, Dalbow, Helms, Erickson, Sinnickson, Hendrickson, Vannaman and Lock. These Swedish-Americans, as well as later Swedes in the area, follow generally the custom of the earlier Swedes by crossing the Delaware for the continued observance of Swedish ways. They attend Swedish Lutheran Churches in and around Philadelphia and belong to the Swedish Colonial Society. Many have joined the Swedish singing societies in Philadelphia.

The folk dances, native songs and other customs of Sweden which are now observed throughout the State were for the most part brought to New Jersey by first generation

Swedes of recent origin, rather than preserved through the centuries by the descendants of the original pioneers. Thus, most of the Swedish life in the State is actually concentrated in the northern region, for of 29,849 residents of Swedish birth or of Swedish parentage, approximately 90 percent now dwell north of Burlington County, the historical boundary of New Sweden in New Jersey. About 70 percent of the Swedish population lives in cities of more than 10,000 population, while an even greater percentage is found in the five metropolitan counties of Hudson, Essex, Bergen, Passaic and Union. Swedish immigrants and their children are today obviously city dwellers, for the largest numbers live in Jersey City, Newark, East Orange and Montclair.

In 1930 the State had 2,271 native and 2,233 first generation Finns. More than half of both groups lived in metropolitan Bergen and Hudson Counties; about one-third of the total was in Jersey City and Teaneck. In addition to these counties, only Essex, Union and Camden had more than 100 of each group.

As Swedish immigration to New Jersey increased, the Swedes soon felt the need of establishing their own churches. While they were not delayed in this achievement so long as their eighteenth century ancestors, it was not until 1889 that the first modern Swedish Lutheran Church was founded in the State. This was Evangelical Lutheran Trinity Church in Dover. The following year churches were organized in Arlington and Jersey City.

Throughout the rest of the decade up to 1900, Swedish Lutheran churches continued to be founded in Essex County. Houses of Lutheran worship were established in East Orange (1893), Montclair (1895), Summit (1897) and Newark (1897). In 1893 there also were founded Swedish Lutheran Churches at Clifton, Paterson and Passaic in Passaic County. Soon after the turn of the century, churches were organized in Plainfield (1901), Elizabeth (1901), West New York (1902) and Bayonne (1903). Others followed at Ridgefield Park in 1906, Englewood in 1909, Bergenfield in 1910 and New Brunswick in 1915.

Swedish notched log construction, visible today in the cabin rebuilt at Salem

Swedish stamps issued for the tercentenary celebration

SWEDES AND FINNS AS AMERICANS

The most recent Swedish Lutheran church is the Bethel Lutheran congregation of Jersey City, founded in 1923.

In 1938, as three centuries ago, the church plays an important role in the lives of Swedish-Americans. And, as two centuries ago, it is the chief repository of Swedish culture, the focal point for the preservation of the Swedish language and customs. Many of the Swedish churches of the State conduct services in Swedish and English and hold observances in the manner of churches in Sweden.

The service of the Swedish Lutheran Churches in the main follows "The Swedish Mass" as it is celebrated in Sweden and dates back to the Swedish reformer, Olavus Petri, who codified the service in 1531. The English translation is considered an exceptionally faithful one. The introits and melodies used are distinctively Swedish; several originated from *Bjuråkers Handskrift*, prior to 1550. The prayers and confessions are direct translations of the Swedish, as are the salutations and responses. Among the typically Swedish customs are the silent prayers at the beginning and close of the service, standing during the reading of the Scriptures, and the extent of congregational singing. Every high mass includes four hymns sung by the congregation.

The Swedish Lutheran church buildings represent a compromise between the strict cross effect of the Episcopal design and the free style of church architecture. Unlike the Episcopalians, the Swedish Lutherans have often placed the pulpit and choir loft outside the sanctuary proper. The churches vary little in design, the positions of pulpit, organ and choir being quite uniform.

A number of typically Swedish festivals are celebrated by the Swedish Lutheran Churches of the State. Perhaps the most characteristic are those centering around Christmas, Julafton and Julotta. The former is Christmas eve and the latter Chritsmas matins. The morning service is always opened with a traditional Swedish hymn written in 1814 especially for this occasion, *All Hail to Thee, O Blessed Morn*.

Julafton is the traditional home evening for the Swedish people. They eat the Christmas eve supper of "lutfisk and gröt" (fish and rice porridge) and exchange gifts. Other families prepare a more elaborate meal of typical Swedish dishes among which are brown beans, meat balls, various types of cheeses, herring prepared in a number of native ways, rice cooked in milk, and assorted cookies and breads. A custom associated with the Christmas meal is that of placing a bean in the rice which indicates to the one who receives it in his portion that he will be married during the coming year.

During the Lenten season some churches observe the Semla Festival in which buns are cut open and filled with almond paste, and then eaten with hot or cold milk poured over them. Known as "semla bullar," this confection has been brought to America from Sweden.

A festival rooted in religion and folklore is Midsummer's Day, marking the summer solstice. In addition to the special significance of the longest day of the year in the Land of the Midnight Sun, the festival is also associated with the Christian observance of the feast of John the Baptist. Also an ancient Swedish custom is the Lucia Fest, which falls on December 13. The main rite is the choice of a young girl to represent St. Lucia. Adorned with a special headdress with candles, she serves coffee to those present. A custom which has developed among the Swedes in America is White Gift Sunday, on which the children and young people bring food, clothes, toys and money to the church on the Sunday prior to Christmas. These gifts, which are distributed to the poor, are placed on a white sheet which signifies the purity of the central message of Christmas.

The Swedish Evangelical Lutheran Church, first Swedish church in New Jersey, is today the largest of the Swedish churches, numbering 15 congregations with 2,124 communicants and 751 children. While there is no official connection between the Swedish Lutheran Churches of New Jersey and the Consistory at Uppsala, cordial reciprocal relations have been maintained. American pastors take part by invitation in the conferences conducted by

SWEDES AND FINNS AS AMERICANS 111

the Swedish church, and there is an interchange of scholars between the two bodies. Although the present Swedish Lutheran Churches are not lineal descendants of the Raccoon church founded by Tollstadius in 1703, the relationship between the churches of this country and the Consistory is, in the words of a Swedish Lutheran minister, "that of the child weaned away from the parent, but on cordial and friendly terms with the parent."

The eighteenth century English influence has a present-day echo in the establishment of other Swedish denominational churches which originated from branches of English Protestantism. The Swedish Methodist Church has congregations in East Orange, Arlington and Jersey City. These three have a voting membership of 250, about 150 more under membership age, and nearly 500 others who maintain some informal connection. There are Swedish Baptist Churches in Montclair, Newark and Arlington, with about 323 members. The Swedish Evangelical Mission Convenant, with ministers at East Orange, North Plainfield, Dover and Montclair (the latter two are Congregationalist), has about 420 members, excluding those at Perth Amboy, where services are held occasionally.

The Salvation Army at Montclair and Arlington, in charge of Swedish officers, is especially active among the Swedes in those communities. The branch in Montclair, which began its work in 1906 and acquired its own building in 1911, conducts all meetings, except those for young people, in Swedish, and most of the children in the Sunday School have Swedish parents.

Several secular organizations have been founded for the furtherance of Swedish culture and traditions. The International Order of Good Templars, a temperance education brotherhood, has five Swedish lodges in New Jersey, situated in East Orange, Roseland, Newark, Jersey City and Westfield. The Swedish Folk Festival Society of the Oranges was formed in 1934 to stimulate interest and participation in Swedish folk dancing, songs, games and related activities. This group also sponsors Swedish exhibits in schools, clubs and churches. The largest Swedish organization in the State is the Vasa Order of America, which has 22 lodges with 2,300 members. Primarily a sick benefit society, its meetings are also devoted to Swedish dancing and music. The Viking Lodge, which maintains 6 chapters in the State, is a similar institution.

The lay center of Swedish activity in New Jersey is the coeducational school of Upsala College at East Orange. Founded in 1893 and operated by the Swedish Lutheran Church, approximately one-third of its 402 students are of Swedish extraction. More than half of the members of the faculty are Swedish. Courses are offered in Swedish language, literature and cultural history.

Named after the great Swedish university at Uppsala, the school was organized by that part of the Augustana Synod which now comprises the New York and New England Conferences. It was originally in Brooklyn, where it was known as the Upsala Institute of Learning; in 1898 it was moved to Kenilworth, N. J., where it remained until 1924, when it was established in East Orange.

Although Upsala is technically a denominational school, neither the curriculum nor the student body is sectarian. A recent survey shows that the highest percentage of students was Catholic, while the next highest was Jewish. The majority of the enrollment is from New Jersey.

In addition to its Swedish Lutheran atmosphere and background, Upsala has two organizations to further interest in Swedish activities. The Swedish Literary Society "De Nio" (The Nine), founded in 1905, meets monthly to discuss phases of Swedish literature and to promote the use of the Swedish language. About ten years ago it became a local chapter of the Swedish Cultural Society, the American branch of the Swedish national group. There is also the Swedish Society, an undergraduate organization whose members meet to converse in Swedish.

The Swedish Cultural Society of Northern New Jersey was organized in 1931 as another chapter of the national society. It meets monthly during the school year, usually at Upsala. It has arranged lectures by both Swedish and American speakers on Sweden's art, architecture,

"Old Main," classroom building at Upsala College, East Orange, N. J.

culture, history, literature, music, schools and cooperatives; and exhibitions of Swedish folk dancing and the Ling system of gymnastics.

Alumni of Upsala have won distinction in a variety of fields, notably in missionary, religious, professional and business spheres. A large number of the students prepare for teaching or business careers. A significant illustration of the secular character of the institution is the decline in the percentage of pastors among the graduates. In 1905 three out of four alumni became ministers, while in 1935 only two out of 62 graduates are listed as members of the clergy.

Three hundred years after the founding of New Sweden, Swedish culture perhaps plays a greater role than ever before in the lives of the people of New Jersey. Yet this has resulted more from direct importation from Sweden than from growth on local soil over three centuries. New Jersey, in common with the rest of the country, feels a number of definite Swedish influences in many aspects of its cultural and commercial life.

On a purely popular basis, the most widespread current Swedish influence is gastronomic. Twenty years ago a Swedish restaurant with smörgåsbord was a novelty even in New York. Today Kungsholms, Valhallas and Stockholms have sprung up in several of the State's larger cities and along the highway. The blue and gold flag which once floated over southern New Jersey flies again, albeit over a restaurant which turns Americans into Swedes for a night.

More profound, however, is the influence that Swedish arts have had latterly on home decoration. Swedish glass and Swedish silver have become extremely popular both as collectors' items and as articles for daily use. The past decade has similarly witnessed a sharp trend toward Swedish design in household furniture, especially sofas and tables.

It is in economics and politics that Sweden enjoys its greatest prestige. In unspectacular fashion, almost unobtrusively, Sweden's consumer and producer cooperatives have stimulated the growth of similar organizations in this country. To thousands of members of New Jersey cooperatives, Sweden represents the modern example in cooperative living. And to thousands more, as well, Marquis W. Childs' *Sweden: The Middle Way* is the most popular work on the subject. Similarly, individuals whose interest in cooperatives may be no greater than academic regard Sweden as the inspiration of the cooperative way.

The growth of appreciation of Sweden's cooperatives has quite logically led to an inquiry by Americans into the nature of the people and government of Sweden. Democratic America has made in the twentieth century a discovery almost as important as that which Sweden itself made in America three hundred years ago. Across the Atlantic, in the cradle of New Sweden, in the land of the imperious Printz and the adventurous Tollstadius, it has found a true sister state—a stronghold of democracy.

XV

SWEDESBORO

UP THE creeks that flow into Delaware River, through a rough, boggy country that could not support cart wheels and sucked at foot travelers, the Swedes came to New Jersey. Seven of these creeks, wide and full flowing enough to be called rivers, served as highways to the new settlements and to the large farms scattered along the banks.

Of the settlements, Raccoon (now Swedesboro) became the most important. It is likely that some of the first Swedes in New Jersey sailed their small boats into Raccoon Creek because of its proximity to the center of Swedish affairs on the west bank of the Delaware. Exactly when they first came is knowledge buried with them in their unknown graves. The Indians called the stream Memiraco or Narraticon, and the Swedes adapted the former name to Araratcung, Ratcung and finally Raccoon or Raccuun.

Governor Peter Holländer Ridder bought the area from Cape May to Raccoon Creek in 1640 and 1641, and the territory above the creek to Mantua Creek was purchased in 1649 by Governor Printz. By 1677 Swedes had settled about the stream and built houses and cowsheds. As early as 1668, however, permission had been granted to a group of Swedes from the Pennsylvania side of the Delaware to purchase land in the area.

As the soil on the west bank wore out and the cattle fodder grew skimpy, more families moved across the Delaware and the population of the Raccoon Creek area increased. But still the farms were too widespread to constitute a town. The greatest single contribution to the centralization of the region was the building of Kings Highway, which today serves as the town's main thoroughfare. Construction of the highway was provided for by the General Assembly sitting at Burlington in 1681, but the road was not completed to Raccoon until about 21 years later. The highway was a major reason for the choice of Raccoon as the site of the first Swedish church in New Jersey, and the church, in turn, attracted settlers from the outlying districts. The road was built both from the north and the south; the southern half reached the settlement about 1702, providing easy access for the settlers from below Raccoon Creek.

Increased population led to agitation for a church on the Jersey side of the Delaware. The Jersey Swedes had been helping to support the parishes at Wicacoa (Philadelphia) and Christina (Wilmington). But the chief contributions of the New Jersey Swedes at meetings of the west shore parishioners were complaints about the cost of ferry fare, the difficulty of the journey, and the time lost from working in the fields. The Jerseymen also feared that their investment in the Pennsylvania churches would be completely lost should they grow numerous enough to support a minister on their own side of the river. Especially insistent were these arguments when a new church was planned for Christina in 1697. As inducements to continue the *status quo*, the Christina Swedes promised to repay the New Jersey members fully should they become strong enough to set up a separate church and support a minister. In addition, the west bank Swedes furnished a canoe "for them to use whenever they come to church, but to be used for no other purpose. If it be lost they [the Jerseyites] shall provide another themselves."

The canoe served not only to carry people to church but to bring to the Rev. Eric Björk, the Christina pastor, their increasingly categorical demands for a church in New Jersey. Pledges of money and materials for building the church at Christina were insufficient, and attendance there fell off. The New Jersey Swedes received an important concession in 1701 when Pastor Björk delegated part of his authority to Hans Stålt, who had been engaged as schoolmaster at Raccoon. Stålt, hired for a year, was directed to hold services, and the people were advised to attend. But the combined school and church which functioned with Björk's approval seems to have been short-lived, and it was certainly ineffective.

Björk's approval of Stålt seems to have been designed to consolidate his own position among the separatists on the New Jersey shore. Jealous of his flock and income, Björk was worried by the activities of Lars Tollstadius. This "priest," without a commission from the head of the Swedish Lutheran church at Uppsala, had been attempting to form a church in New Jersey by combining the interests of the Swedes who belonged to Björk's parish at Christina and those attached to the Wicacoa church. Tollstadius gained headway, and Björk made repeated visits to the Jersey settlements to convince his parishioners who lived below Raccoon Creek not to join with the Wicacoa flock from above the creek in a new church. From Tollstadius he extracted a promise to stop preaching among the Christina church parishioners.

Tollstadius broke his word, however, and the settlers from New Jersey were "mostly indifferent and tardy in coming over to church." The church at Raccoon was built in 1703—a little log buliding close to Kings Highway, near where the present Trinity Church stands. In the early fall of that year Tollstadius preached the dedicatory sermon. The building was erected on a plot purchased from John Hugg, a Quaker. Shortly after the founding of the parish, the land holdings of the church totaled 100 acres. The property, exclusive of the church plot and the burial ground, offered a source of income in ground rents. The land was leased *in perpetuo,* could be transferred by the original lessees, but could be seized by the church for non-payment of the quitrent. Although the rents have not been paid for many years, Trinity Church still has the right to collect them.

Björk and Dean Sandel of the Wicacoa church never gave up hope of bringing the Jersey Swedes back to their parishes. Accordingly, when in 1706 "there arose a shameful report about Herr Tolstadius, that he had a child with a girl in Rattcong [Raccoon] Creek, Olle Parson's unmarried daughter Catharine, which proved more and more true," the west shore parsons increased their efforts to break the separatist front. Tollstadius was bound over to the Burlington court, but before that body met his corpse was washed up on the Pennsylvania shore. His canoe had been found 9 days earlier. In his journal, after his report of Tollstadius' death, Björk mentions that the Raccoon people were "more obstinate and spunky than ever."

The Rev. Jonas Aurén, who succeeded Tollstadius, had come to New Sweden with Björk and Rudman. For a time he had conducted services for the English at Elk River and had continuously put off his return to Sweden. With Aurén came Carl Brunjen, a relative who had been a schoolmaster in Sweden. In the latter part of 1706 Brunjen established a school in Raccoon on property which, according to the original deed, may be used only for educational purposes. One of Swedesboro's grammar schools stands on the site of the tiny log building, close to the church.

Björk was far more sympathetic to Aurén than to Tollstadius. When Aurén, at the insistence of the Raccoon Swedes, was granted permission by Governor Cornbury to act as their minister, Björk, cognizant of Aurén's Adventist sympathies, agreed, but advised Aurén to be "circumspect and careful in what he did." Aurén was to confine his efforts to a limited area and not to encroach on Björk's private churchyard, for, as Björk said, "he has already gotten a bit of my bread . . . and therefore he should let the remainder alone."

For 7 years, until his death, Aurén preached at Raccoon, traveled occasionally to outlying sections as was the custom, and waited patiently for the parishioners to pay his salary.

The church united the families who worked cooperatively for its welfare. Building and repairing, discussions of finance, divine services and general meetings knit the broad area into a community conscious of its unity. Important to the church was the education and welfare of the children. The establishment of the school on church property at Raccoon centralized the interests of the young people, and the church choir further brought the families together.

After the death of Aurén in 1713, the Swedish parishioners in New Jersey finally persuaded the Swedish Lutheran Consistory at Uppsala to appoint a pastor for the region. The church officials named the Rev. Abraham Lidenius. Like his two predecessors, he continually importuned his congregation to pay his salary, provide funds for repairing the church and burial ground, and make good on other pledges. Cash was limited; food, materials and labor generally had to suffice as payments. Lidenius complained often and at length about the hardships which were his. Finally it was decided to collect all the contributions and pay him at the half year. When this was done, the total was less than £8. At a meeting with the parishioners, Lidenius again described "his miserable condition" and said that he "would have to suffer hunger and nakedness unless his condition were improved." He threatened to leave the congregation, but since he did receive food he remained.

In 1723 an agreement was signed by 52 members of the church pledging varying amounts toward the pastor's support. Lidenius remarked that some did not sign the paper because "they did not want to." Gabriel Peterson pledged more to the parish than others, but it cannot be inferred from this that he was the wealthiest Swede in the district, since in a previous request for funds "Hermanus Helm, who has 100 pounds put out at interest, promised 36 shillings, while Månne Didricsson, who has a hard enough time making his living, both promised and gave more."

A new vestibule, porch and fireplaces were planned for the church. Repairs were made on the burial ground fence, which, because of its dilapidation, permitted "swine and everything" to roam the consecrated ground at will. The "and everything" perhaps referred to ghouls who, as later reports show, were constantly robbing the graves.

The leaders of the Swedish church spent much of their

time working at the building and collecting money from the other parishioners. The names of the Helms, Mattssons, Petersons, Locks, Hoffmans, Cocks and Dalbos appear again and again in the lists of those who were charged with specific duties at parish meetings. Åke (Israel) Helm served for many years as leading vestryman and general collector of funds. Others of the congregation undertook tasks which ranged from building benches for the choir and plastering the broken walls of the church to buying horses and cattle for the ministers. But despite the efforts of some members, the church did not prosper, and the ministers' requests for salaries came almost with the regularity of their sermons.

Lidenius had pleaded strenuously with the church members to purchase living quarters for him and had accomplished his purpose by insistent reiteration and threat of departure. At one time when the glebe, or parsonage farm, was discussed, Lidenius read the congregation a letter from Queen Ulrica announcing a shipment of Bibles and hymn books for the New Sweden settlers because of their "steadfastness" in maintaining their faith. But Lidenius could find reason only to remonstrate against the "hardness and blindness" of his congregation.

In February 1724 the last parish meeting with Lidenius as pastor was attended by 54 persons. The plaster on the exterior of the church was falling off, and the pigs still roamed the graveyard.

For about 2 years after Lidenius was transferred, the Raccoon church had no regular ordained minister. There is no record of parish meetings or services. But since baptisms and marriages were entered in the church record, the congregation probably was served by lay pastors and occasional visits from the clergy across the river. In 1726, however, Peter Tranberg was installed as the pastor of Raccoon and began his work of rehabilitating the neglected parish.

But Tranberg's accomplishments were few. The parishioners' lack of interest necessitated a resolution which delegated power to the vestrymen and wardens. These officials,

Interior of Trinity Church, Swedesboro

too, found difficulty in collecting members' pledges for the support of the church, the pastor's salary and the reconstruction of the glebe, which the people of Raccoon supported jointly with those of Penns Neck. In 1727 this was excessively burdensome, for "the hard winter which was that year threw both the ministers and the members of the congregation into straightened circumstances." Lack of money was accompanied by a seeming lack of interest of the people in services, which they showed by running in and out of the church during the sermon.

During the first 2 years of Tranberg's tenure, 24 persons, or almost half the church membership, failed to make their pledged contributions. Like the earlier ministers, Tranberg theatened to leave, and the threat moved the congregation to fulfill its promise. Still there was enough money in the treasury in 1730 to purchase a £7 silver goblet and paten, which are still used. In an effort to bolster attendance and interest, a special gallery for young people was contracted for, but even this did not seem effective.

It was strange, therefore, that when Peter Tranberg was transferred to the church at Christina in 1741 by the Swedish Lutheran Consistory, his Swedish congregation at Raccoon, "which . . . had already rather declined and diminished," opposed this transfer so strenuously. They refused at first to accept Olaf Malander of the Wicacoa parish, who was temporarily to fill the gap. Some weeks elapsed before the stubborn Raccooners rescinded their original resolve "never to have anything to do with any Swedish minister" and accepted Malander. He was received by the majority of the congregation, about 20 families and "almost as many Batchellors."

The number of Swedish families and eligible family heads had scarcely grown in 20 years. The influence of the English was increasing, and Malander, with the approval of the Swedish congregation, began to hold services in English to attract these settlers to the church and insure his greater security. This did not help, and in September of 1742 Malander left, "wishing his successor better fortune." Once again the parish was without a pastor or regular services, the two influences that preserved a community spirit among the widely separated farmers.

The religious Swedes, left with only the semblance of church organization, were fertile soil for the growth of the Moravian movement, founded in Germany by Count von Zinzendorf. Paul Daniel Bryzelius, Swedish by birth, sailed for America in 1741, intending to provide the impoverished sections of South Jersey with religious services. As leader of the Moravian Brotherhood, he came to the pastorless Swedes at Raccoon in the role of missionary.

Bryzelius was so persuasive a proselytizer that he obtained permission of part of the Raccoon congregation to preach in the church there. There were some, however, who vigorously opposed his coming. According to Israel Acrelius, a later Swedish pastor and historian, "a Sunday was appointed for Bryzelius to preach in the Raccoon Church. The people assembled in great numbers—one party to put him in, another to keep him out, and a third to see the fun. But the advantage was on the side of those who were opposed to him for they had the church key..." Some of Bryzelius' supporters broke through a window to open the door from within, but when the door opened, "there was fighting to get in, noise and terrible confusion so that they went away without any service at all, but with great scandal." Bryzelius was later prohibited from preaching at Raccoon by a Gloucester County Court.

A parish meeting was called to depose those church officers who had been attracted to the Moravian doctrine, and Åke (Israel) Helm, Hans Stillman, Gabriel Frenne, Hindric Hindricsson, Joannes Hoffman, Gustav Gustavsson, Lars Lock and Eric Runnels were elected vestrymen and wardens. Gabriel Näsman, the Wicacoa pastor, thereafter held occasional services in the church, but peripatetic Moravians still preached at private homes. The religious dispute dispelled the calm that had been broken by nothing more serious than the repetitious requests for funds. Those still loyal to the Swedish Lutheran church petitioned the Consistory for a new pastor, but the Moravians, no doubt attracted by the offer of £30 sterling made in the petition, sent Abraham Reinicke, another Swedish-born Moravian, to the parish before the slow-moving Consistory could consider a decision. Reinicke, "on account of the novelty," at first attracted a large attendance. But he did not last long. Acrelius suggests that one reason why the Raccoon people tired of him was that at funeral services he kept them "so long with prayers and preaching, that if the people had not stopped him they would not have had daylight to get to the graveyard."

The Swedish Consistory was sufficiently worried about Raccoon to appoint Johan Sandin to the vacant pastorate in 1748, with instructions to check the anti-Swedish Lutheran movement and the growing disregard for the Swedish language. So important was this problem considered by the Uppsala authorities that they made Sandin not only pastor of the Raccoon parish, but also Dean of the entire Swedish Lutheran Church in America. Sandin could accomplish little before his death 5 months later. Peter Kalm, the naturalist and historian, halted his travels long enough to fill in as lay pastor. His letter to the Consistory on behalf of the congregation resulted in the selection of an ordained minister.

The Rev. Eric Unander, who had come to America with Israel Acrelius, the new Dean, was temporarily appointed to take Sandin's place. The appointment was made permanent when the church members petitioned the Consistory to keep the "regular pastor . . . Mr. Unander whom we, in our simplicity, have learned to regard as very learned."

But the Swedish language needed more than one hypodermic to keep it alive in Raccoon. Disturbed by the fact that the church records at the Raccoon church were being kept in English, Dean Acrelius ordered that Swedish be used, although he permitted the use of Latin script.

In 1755 Unander was succeeded by Johan Abraham Lidenius, the church's first American-born pastor and the son of Abraham Lidenius, the earlier pastor. Lidenius, in turn, was followed by the Rev. Johan Wicksell, whose limited English did not satisfy his parishioners at Raccoon.

In their homes and in church they wished to hear English; this outspoken desire and common practice constantly gnawed into the weakened cord of Swedish authority. In one last desperate effort to maintain its influence, the Swedish Consistory appointed to the Raccoon pulpit Nicholas Collin, a brilliant young scholar, who combined with his religion a grasp of the political problems soon to precipitate the Revolution. The parish had been granted an English charter in 1765, and was clamoring for services in English. Collin began them in 1770.

In the 70 years since the founding of the church, Raccoon had drawn closer to Kings Highway, concentrated its homes, and become an important stagecoach stop. Along Raccoon Creek dikes had been erected to prevent flooding of the low meadowland where the cattle grazed. The sandy soil was not particularly good for agriculture, although great quantities of corn were planted. Masons, carpenters, millers and weavers lived in the settlement and often worked on community enterprises.

In the days of the Rev. Wicksell there must have been enough Swedish homes to give the settlement the appearance of a village, for he gave it the name "Swedesborough," built a rectory in 1764, and in 1771 wrote a lease which specified "free schooling forever." The rectory was a cedar log structure, afterward weather-boarded to resemble an ordinary frame house. The school, too, was built of logs.

The village was a parade ground for both British and American forces during the early years of the Revolution. The opposing troops foraged in and around the district and, on occasion, established headquarters in the village. Twice during the hostilities, Dr. Collin narrowly escaped hanging by the Colonials when he was taken prisoner. Accused of aiding the British cause, he was forced to occupy "a small corner of one room" in the parsonage. Collin always insisted that he was a "foreign spectator," and it is known that he aided the wounded of both sides. In 1778 the one-room schoolhouse was destroyed by the British, who claimed that Tories had been imprisoned there. There is a legend that the church would have suffered the same fate except that Dr. Collin, dressed in ecclesiastical robes similar to those worn by Church of England rectors, was conducting a funeral in the churchyard and was mistaken for an Episcopal minister.

Church services were interrupted during the course of the war because the British feared that sermons preached in foreign languages might be seditious, and because the church at times was army headquarters. A division of American troops stationed in Swedesboro in 1778 "filled the church with filth and vermin so that it could not be used for divine services."

As elsewhere, sentiment at Swedesboro was divided on the American cause. Records exist to show that Swedesboro Swedes were taken to New York as British prisoners for their anti-English activity, revealing that the town had its Colonial supporters. On the other hand, Dr. Collin writes of the "husband of a Swedish woman," accused of trading with the English. Tied to a tree near the church by the Colonials, he was beaten with a stick until his body was "crushed and cut up. Several days later he died."

The outstanding Revolutionary to stop at Swedesboro was General "Mad Anthony" Wayne, whose successful foraging trip to supply the army at Valley Forge during the winter of 1777-78 gave rise to the phrase still spoken by lower New Jersey residents, "South Jersey cattle saved the Nation." One midnight, with the British hot on his tracks, he sought the comparative safety of the rectory at Swedesboro. He left early the following morning, just a few moments before the pursuing British arrived.

When the armies marched to the north, the rebuilding of the schoolhouse began. Collin, however, turned his energies toward a task much closer to his heart: the erection of a new church.

For nearly 80 years the old log structure had served the Raccoon region, and it was considered unsafe. Within a few weeks Collin was able to obtain pledges in excess of £1,400. Contracts were signed in 1783 and work began in the spring. Collin acted as a kind of construction supervisor, arranging for workmen, inspecting each brick. After trenches had been dug for the foundation, it was decided that the 50- by 40-foot plan was too small "to allow the number and form of the windows and other parts of the plan which were indispensable for convenience, symmetry and neat elegance." Collin then re-planned the building on a larger scale.

The work was slowed down in the fall, "the season proving very sickly." Nevertheless the exterior was finished by Christmas, and in the following year (1784) the church was opened for a congregation not only of Swedes but also of Dutch, Germans, English, and even a Negro family.

This multinational character of the first congregation proved an omen. Only 2 years later the parish changed its allegiance as well as its name. English domination was recognized as a fact when the Swedish Evangelical Lutheran Church became the Trinity Episcopal Church in 1786. Collin was asked to remain as pastor of the congregation until an ordained Episcopal minister could be obtained. With his removal to Philadelphia in 1787, the official Swedish influence disappeared from the parish, although Collin continued to visit the New Jersey church occasionally.

To the newly designated Episcopalians went the responsibility of completing the building. Although Collin had collected £1,310 of the £1,418 pledged—a percentage that no doubt would have been considered miraculous by his half-starved predecessors—it was found that a larger amount was needed. Collections lagged after Collin left, and it was not until 1791 that the church was finished at a cost of £1,928.

Swedesboro had grown slightly during the first half of the eighteenth century as a result of increased stagecoach traffic. This growth, as it continued, in addition to intermarriage lessened the Swedish character of the community. No organization held the Swedish population together; no reason existed to continue the old traditions. The travelers who stopped here were mainly Englishmen from Philadelphia or Salem, or from northern and central New Jersey and New York.

Toward the end of the eighteenth century, Swedesboro

Swedesboro, Kings Highway, a section of the business district

had but a dozen log dwellings, a schoolhouse, a parsonage and a tavern; but by 1830 there were 64 houses, 5 stores, 2 hotels, 2 tailor shops, harness and carriage shops, a blacksmithy, fulling mills and gristmills. The number of church communicants had grown since affiliation with the Episcopal Church, and additions were made to the rectory and the church proper.

The hundred years of Swedesboro's history after 1805 were spanned by the life of one man, John Pierson, of Swedish extraction. Pierson, who was born in 1805, served in county and State positions for 39 years. He encouraged the growth of his town by constructing 83 bridges, many of them across the creeks which cut Kings Highway.

On land still owned by the church, and upon which the church may still collect ground rents, the business section of Swedesboro was built. Although the population has increased less than 650 during the past 30 years to reach a total of 2,213, the gradual growth has required the building of new schools. Swedesboro now has three elementary schools and one high school. Two large plants, a canning factory and a basket factory, operate all year and give employment not only to Swedesboro residents but also to those from surrounding areas.

Swedesboro does not reveal its history at a glance. The town's directory lists few names that recall its origin. Broad, macadamized Kings Highway little resembles the rather narrow dirt road that was the original backbone of the town. Nor do the frame houses suggest the log cabins of the early Swedes who lived about Raccoon Creek. Only the name of the village and quiet Trinity Church, half-surrounded by its old graveyard, speak of things that were.

Perched on four thin legs, close to the white spire of Trinity Church, the silvered water tank of a canning company rises over its low, wide, dark buildings. One-family stucco or frame houses, set in wide lawns and gardens, are painted light yellow or tan, occasionally white, and give the village a bright, 7-o'clock-on-a-sunny-morning look. Most of the houses were built before the World War. Many have the wide porches and gingerbread decorations of the Victorian period, and some display old-fashioned iron grillwork.

The retired farmers who make up a large proportion of Swedesboro's population expect the apothecary to sell drugs, penny candy, and no sandwich lunches—and that is what he sells. The housewives like to shop out of the rain and sun, so many of the stores have metal canopies.

In addition to its own residents, Swedesboro serves the farmers of the surrounding agricultural belt. During the tomato or asparagus season hundreds of trucks are backed up to the curb on Railroad Avenue, just behind Kings Highway, and here the growers sell their produce to the buyers from Philadelphia and New York. On Saturdays, all through the year, the village is the general store and amusement center for these same farmers whose trucks and cars crowd the streets, from noon until 11 o'clock when the movies are out. Harness, fertilizer, poultry feed and bags of seed are displayed on the wide, clean streets. The cashiers of the two banks know their depositors well enough to call most of them by their first names.

Trinity Episcopal Church, Kings Highway and Church St., is still occasionally called "Old Swedes Church." The mellowed, red brick structure follows the architectural plan of the later Georgian work of New England and Pennsylvania. Gracefully arched, many-mullioned windows with neat wood trim and keys over the old brickwork are, like the side entrance doors, touched with the classic ornament of the Grecian Revival period. The great, ivy-colored brick tower with its somewhat awkward wooden steeple was erected in 1838.

The white woodwork of the bright interior is strongly marked by the classic revival style, but the old arrangement of balcony and box pews remains. Alterations which revamped the decorations above the altar and placed a baptismal font unsymmetrically at the side have removed much of the original naïve charm. Only a few feet from the site of the original log building, the church is set in a graveyard which stretches down to Raccoon Creek. Some of the headstones have old Swedish names: the Hendricksons, Homans, Helms, Dalbos and others.

XVI

PENNS NECK

CONTRARY to the usual practice of Swedish and Finnish immigrants, the colonists who came to Penns Neck left their boats on the shore of the Delaware, settling there or moving slowly overland to the interior. Their legacy to contemporary New Jersey is the tiny village of Churchtown, the original center of activities that spread for approximately 15 miles along the Delaware between Oldmans Creek and Varkens Kill (Salem Creek). Churchtown presents an indiscriminate collection of light-colored, dull frame houses dotting the highway that runs through what should be the town center. But there is no center—not even a small moving picture house to attract farmers on Saturdays. Most of the 50 residents work in the nearby plants of du Pont and the Atlantic City Electric Company, visit the larger towns in the vicinity occasionally or make trips to Philadelphia. Churchtown itself serves as a quiet interlude.

The village is of relatively recent development. The original settlers made no attempt to form a compact community but built individual homes on large tracts providing ample space for crops and cattle. Records of land purchases by the Swedes and Finns date back to 1676, but undoubtedly the settlers had come long before. It is believed that Finnish colonists located in the Penns Neck area about 1660, or perhaps earlier.

On the flat, lonely point jutting into Delaware River, where occasional farmhouses break the monotony and the high earthworks of dismantled Fort Mott block off the river view, no sign remains of the original settlers whose nationality lingers in the name "Finns Point." The community, built on the most westerly point in New Jersey, was called Lampanshouck by the Dutch; the English named it Finns Towne Point, suggesting by this name that there must have been a certain homogeneity about the place when the Englishman Fenwick came to this area in 1675. On a map of 1685 the territory is referred to as Finns' Land, and a small creek dividing Upper and Lower Penns Neck is marked as Finnish on the same map. Deeds show that in 1689 Stephen Yerians and Lasse Hendricks, both Finns, each owned 250 acres at Finns Point.

A fort built here by the early settlers has gone with the Finns. Its exact location, its form or plan, have never been discovered. On the approximate site, overlooking the Delaware, the United States has erected a memorial to the Confederate soldiers who died in the Union prison on a nearby island.

The Swedes for the most part settled to the north of Finns Point, though others scattered southward along the shore of Salem Cove. Quaker occupation checked Swedish and Finnish penetration to the east. The Shutes, Johnsons, Neilsons, Mattisons, Sinicksons, Andersons, Danielsons and other Swedes owned land hereabouts before 1680. They mingled with the Dutch, English, French and German colonists, but through their church activities the Swedes and Finns managed to keep their identity well on into the eighteenth century. In a list of 46 taxable persons in the district in 1676, 19 were Swedes or Finns.

The New Jersey settlers from the west side of the Delaware continued as members of the Wicacoa (Philadelphia) or Christina (Wilmington) parishes, depending on the location of their new homes. The Penns Neck Swedes and Finns came under the jurisdiction of Pastor Björk of the Christina church. Like the settlers in the Raccoon area, these people also resented the hard trip overland and across the river to attend church. They joined their Raccoon brothers in a separatist movement that worried Pastor Björk, who was partly dependent upon their financial support. The separatists finally won certain concessions from the Christina parish.

Perhaps the most important of these concessions was Björk's approval of a plan to reimburse his Penns Neck parishioners when they should become sufficiently numerous to support a parish of their own. "When they . . .

should become so strong as to be able to set up a separate church and procure and support a minister . . . the people from Christina would help them with money again as much as they now help towards building this church at Christina," said Björk. But later events showed just how grudging this concession was. Meanwhile, the Penns Neck Swedes, who held four of the seven places in the vestry of the Christina church, planned stronger action for separation.

After meeting several times with the Swedes and Finns at Penns Neck, Björk was forced to recognize the fact that they were slipping from him. He advised them to attend services in charge of Hans Stålt, the schoolmaster at Raccoon.

When Lars Tollstadius finally succeeded in forming the Raccoon parish and building a church, Björk went into full action to protect his own rights in New Jersey. In a letter he reminded the people "of their obedience" to him and warned them to "heed the shame and injury that their doings would cause in Sweden." This was of no avail, and Björk hastily scuttled across the river to meet with the people there once more. He pointed out that they had agreed to support the Christina church until they were able to form a congregation of their own. In any event, they should not unite with the Raccoon people, "as we have never had anything to do with them, nor they with us in any such business." Angrily, Björk noted that his logic "seemed to weigh with some, but there were found enough stiff-necked and obdurate ones to render it of no avail."

By 1702 New Jersey settlers attending the Christina church services had dwindled to "two or three." This had occurred, Björk thought, "partly on account of the bad ferriage, but mostly perhaps from unwillingness." Once again he called a meeting and insisted that the Penns Neck people were not yet ready for a pastor of their own and that they should "support one well first and pay yearly what they had promised, before they attempt to take another and then deal in like manner with him." To this he added that he "would not suffer them" to do as they pleased with him, and "that if they get ten Priests" without authority from the Swedish Consistory, they must still pay their yearly dues to him.

The meetings continued with a constantly decreasing attendance as Björk boiled, and the Penns Neck parishioners calmly joined forces with the Raccoon people to build a church with Lars Tollstadius as minister. In desperation Björk appealed for support to Wholley Stobey, who had much influence because the people "for the most part were in his debt." This plan had some slight effect, for a number of the Swedes at Penns Neck asked Björk to conduct services occasionally on this side of the river. Björk came over, first to collect what was owing him and then to preach at the home of his loyal parishioner, Jacob Van Dever, where the question of his salary was discussed. Peter Lucasson probably argued against paying him, for Björk states that he "was superlatively foolish . . . and got an answer suitable to the circumstance."

Björk made occasional trips to Penns Neck. But after the Raccoon church was built in 1703, the two New Jersey areas became more closely united at Björk's expense. They first shared Tollstadius and then Jonas Aurén, who had come from Sweden with Björk. Since there was no church at Penns Neck, services were held in centrally situated homes. This arrangement was not altogether satisfactory, and the Swedes at Penns Neck continued their agitation for an independent parish and permission to build a church.

The permission was ultimately granted in 1713 when Björk, who had become Dean of the Swedish Lutheran Churches in America, finally yielding to the Penns Neck parishioners after his transfer from the Christina parish, so recommended to the head of the Swedish Consistory. The parishioners had been united in battle for more than 15 years, yet when the time came to erect the church in Penns Neck, they could not agree on a site. At a parish meeting in 1714 "it was finally decided, after much difficulty, to build . . . down by the river" at the ferry station, where the German members of the newly formed congregation had their burial ground. Nine months later nothing

St. George Episcopal Church, Churchtown, erected 1811 near site of Penns Neck Swedish Church, founded 1714

had been accomplished. At this time, however, unanimity as to location was achieved when Jean Jaquet, a French Huguenot member of the congregation, donated the 4 acres of land on which the present church stands, "for the consideration of the love and good will I bear toward my loving friends and neighbors here in Pennsneck."

Work on the building continued until May 1715, when it was once more suspended for 9 months. Then, in another spurt of activity, the entire congregation assisted the carpenters who had been hired to make the roof. By the following October the floor had been laid, and in January 1717 plans were made for completing the work, including the pews.

Together with permission to build the church, the parishioners at Penns Neck obtained the services of the Rev. Abraham Lidenius, whose persistence and sincerity were chiefly responsible for the building. In 1714 he demanded of the Christina congregation the money promised to the Penns Neck congregation. At the meeting in Christina the "obligation was acknowledged just, and . . . none of the Christina congregation could deny that such a transaction had taken place. . . . But unluckily it was found that many of the congregation were much more ready to promise than to fulfill." The money was nominally and circuitously paid in 1727 by canceling a debt which the Penns Neck parish owed for church services to the Rev. Samuel Hesselius, who in turn owed almost as large a sum to the Christina parish. On March 31, 1717, St. George Church was dedicated. About this time a severe epidemic carried off a large proportion of the parishioners, and from that day the church had relatively few communicants.

Until he returned to Sweden in 1724, Lidenius served both the Raccoon and Penns Neck parishes. From time to time he requested money either for his salary or for improvements to the church; complained of the children who made "a dreadful noise outside the church;" begged for a horse so that he could cover his widespread parishes with greater dispatch, and pleaded for the house which had long been promised him.

For 2 years after Lidenius' departure, the Rev. Samuel Hesselius, pastor at Christina, filled in at Raccoon and Penns Neck. In 1726 the Rev. Peter Tranberg was appointed pastor at Raccoon, and the Rev. Andrew Windrufwa was sent to Penns Neck. Windrufwa appears little in the church records, although there is frequent mention of "Mr. Windrufwa's horse," and a major battle occurred over whether the animal belonged to the pastor or the pastorate. The question came up again when Tranberg was appointed to Penns Neck upon Windrufwa's death in 1728. For him, too, the parish bought a horse, but it was decided that he could own it only by dying, for "should he be called to any other congregation, then the horse was to belong to" the Penns Neck parish. To this, however, Raccoon would not agree, and the fate of the animal seems never to have been definitely settled.

When Tranberg was transferred to Christina in 1741, Olaf Malander, a lay preacher, filled the vacancies at the two parishes. Malander left in 1742, and for the next 6 years Penns Neck was without a regular pastor. Occasionally Gabriel Näsman, pastor of the Philadelphia Swedish congregation, came to the east shore of the Delaware "for a suitable reward." But the arrangement was too loose to be effective, and the congregation accepted the Moravian preachers or conducted their services according to the Church of England. The church squabbles precipitated by the Moravian infiltration and by the decision of the Penns Neck people to adhere to the Church of England, came to an end in 1748 when the Consistory sent as pastor for Raccoon and Penns Neck the Rev. Johan Sandin. "A great many of those in Penns Neck had declared that they did not any longer desire to have a Swedish Minister," but they finally accepted him. Sandin's tenure was short-lived; he died 5 months later and Eric Unander replaced him.

Peter Kalm, the Finnish-Swedish naturalist who traveled through America about the middle of the eighteenth century, described the Penns Neck area as "not very hilly . . . and in most places . . . covered with open woods of hardwood trees, especially oak. Now and then you see a single farm, and a little cultivated field around it. Here and there are little marshes and swamps, and sometimes a sluggish brook."

Israel Acrelius, the Dean of the Swedish Lutheran churches in America, also visited Penns Neck at about the same time. He wrote that the section was "as yet but little cleared or inhabitated, the air being unhealthy, and producing chills and fever. Good springs are rarely found, and the people generally have a pale and sickly appearance."

The Finns Point community had all but disappeared by this time. The Finnish language, which formerly had been spoken by the settlers, was no longer used in the vicinity. Most of the Finns were dead, "and their descendants changed into Englishmen." Peter Kalm was given a copy of a Finnish psalmbook which his friend Hermanus Helm believed to be "not only the oldest of all Finnish and Swedish books" in the Colony, but the only one available in that language. This is understandable, since the Finns had no church of their own, worshiping usually with the Swedes at Penns Neck.

Living close to the English, the Swedish settlers more and more adopted English ways. Use of the Swedish tongue became uncommon, and Swedish customs were forgotten. When the Rev. Nicholas Collin visited the parish in 1770, he noted that the congregation was "entirely English."

There was not wholehearted support for the Revolutionary cause in Penns Neck. In 1776 Collin reported that "after the English army . . . spread itself over Jersey, there was constant alarm. Formerly nearly all had been eager to take part, but now as the fire came closer, many drew away, and there was much dissension among the people. Many concealed themselves in the woods, or within their houses, other people were forced to carry arms, others offered opposition and refused to go." One young Penns Neck parishioner barely escaped death when soldiers shot at him after he had refused to join the army.

As he jumped to his horse, the bullet whizzed by and imbedded itself in an oak tree.

The congregation at Penns Neck officially transferred to the Episcopal Church of America before Nicholas Collin left in 1787. Three years later John Wade became the first English rector, and in 1794 St. George Church was incorporated. The building was in very poor condition, and in 1811 the present structure was erected, about 200 yards north of the site of the original log building.

St. George Church, on the NW. corner of US 130 and Church Landing Road, was remodeled in 1877. It is a small, weathered, red brick structure with a tiny wooden belfry and an even smaller chimney beside it. Above the brown-painted entrance is a rose window proportionate to the size of the church. The interior is center-aisled with a vaulted ceiling. There is only one modern note: an oil furnace. The pointed windows are of stained glass, unlike in their color emphasis because they were donated at different times. The church is now a mission of St. John's Episcopal Church of Salem. The services, according to the sexton, "are virtually reunions of the Jaquet family," whose ancestor originally donated the land.

XVII
THE GLEBE

THE Rev. Abraham Lidenius was a patient man. As bachelor pastor of Raccoon parish, he was content to move from family to family in the settlement. But when he married Elizabeth Van Neuman and took charge of the newly formed Penns Neck congregation, Lidenius felt that he was entitled to a suitable parsonage. The people of Raccoon suggested that a house be built on land belonging to their church, but Lidenius objected because there he "could not expect any grain crop." Good land was essential, as he "received too small a salary to live" without the produce from a farm. At a meeting of the two parishes in 1715, it was finally decided that the pastor should take a vacant farm in Penns Neck pending erection of a parsonage.

For 5 years nothing happened. Finally, in January 1720, Måns Kyhn, Peter Lock, Fredrick Hoffman and Michael Laikian were appointed to report on the respective merits of the Raccoon parish land and a plot midway between Raccoon and Penns Neck, belonging to Anders Dalbo. The 4-man committee reported that the Dalbo land was much superior. Dalbo, forced to sell because of numerous debts, had priced his land at £112, but when he heard "that the congregation wanted to buy it, he demanded £150." Though they did not agree at once, the committee finally accepted his price and arranged for signing a contract 2 weeks later.

Meanwhile, however, "Anders Dalbo changed his mind, thinking, undoubtedly, that the congregation was so anxious for his farm that he could get more for it than ever it was worth; wherefore the congregation left off its dealing with him and came to an agreement with George Kyhn to buy his plantation." This land, in what is now the township of Pilesgrove, was purchased for £145. The Glebe, as it was called, lay about midway between the two churches, close to Kings Highway, the main road of the region.

The church records report, with evident satisfaction, that Anders Dalbo "undoubtedly regretted what he had done . . . for not only was he forced to sell his land for £100, but also had to pay interest on the money he owed for two years longer."

Collections were still being made in April 1720. Building operations began in May when logs were cut; 3 months later workmen were hired to erect the building. Members of both congregations and the pastor himself aided in construction, which continued well on into 1721. Some made contributions in the form of work, cutting logs, clearing the swamp, cutting laths and clapboards, and actually raising the building. The house appears from the records to have been a rather large, clapboard structure with dormer windows, a porch and a cellar. The interior had finished woodwork, mantelpieces, probably of brick, and clay stoves. Late in 1721 Lidenius took possession of his 117 acres of ground and his new home.

When Lidenius left for Sweden in 1724, the Glebe was in a down-at-the-heel condition. The congregation decided to repair the fences and put the place in good order, arranging that those "who did not desire to work" should be "assessed five bushels of grain for five days work." When the job was done, they stipulated that "afterwards the one who lived there should keep it up." This arrangement did not work well because the pastors had too much to do, while the members of the congregation were too interested in preserving the value of their investment to let the Glebe deteriorate.

Olaf Malander, an unmarried preacher, refused to make his home at the Glebe, probably because of its lonely situation. At a parish meeting the members of the congregation bid against one another for the right to board the pastor. The lowest bidder won. When the Rev. Johan Sandin arrived 6 years after Malander's departure, the congregation decided that the Glebe should continue to be rented as a source of the pastor's income. This practice did not help the farm, and a new building program became necessary during the Rev. Eric Unander's tenure. At a

Glebe, or Parsonage Farm, near Woodstown

cost of more than £56 a new barn was built and shingled; the cellar was repaired and the house re-covered; doors, chimneys and windows were repaired, so that the Glebe once more became a fit home for a pastor.

By 1764 the Swedish Lutherans were losing ground in Penns Neck and centering their activities in Raccoon. In that year a new rectory was being built in Raccoon, and the congregation searched for a way to pay the £100 asked by the carpenter-contractor. The Rev. Johan Wicksell was prevailed upon to live in Raccoon so that the Glebe could be leased rent-free to the carpenter, John Keen, in payment of his bill. The congregation had all it could do to pay the pastor £20 a year and could not raise the £100 at once. Unwilling to accept installment payments, Keen agreed to accept the Glebe rent-free for 5 years as payment. Beyond the 5-year rent-free period, Keen leased the property for 5 additional years, promising to keep it in good repair during his tenancy. The income from the rent was divided equally between the two parishes of Raccoon and Penns Neck. So favorable was this arrangement that no preacher ever occupied the house again. Sometimes the money collected was put out at interest with some member of the congregations, but usually it helped to pay the pastor's salary. In 1795 the property was sold to Edward Hall for £1,600.

The Glebe, still so called, is a large double building, three stories high, its peaked roofs meeting at right angles to form a T. The newer portion, built in 1850, differs little from the original. Both are of yellow stucco. The porch across the front is ample, easily accommodating the present occupants, an Irish family with 21 children.

The house stands on a knoll about 200 yards from a dirt road between Woodstown and Sharptown. The land here, more rolling than that nearer the Delaware, is tilled in broad fields running back from the roadside to the shadow of scrub forests in the background. The fields on either side of the road are part of the Glebe. It is an open, sunny area, as devoid of homes now as when the old parsonage was built.

XVIII

REPAUPO

THE twenty-odd farmhouses, the gasoline station and country store, ranged in ragged order around a crossroads near Repaupo Creek, are the descendants of New Sweden's most Swedish settlement. It is not known just when the size of the early settlement entitled it to a name, but there undoubtedly were Swedes in the area when Cornelis Learson, Ole Rasen and Ole Jonson received purchase rights from the English Governor Philip Carteret in 1668.

These men transferred their options to Hans Hopman, Peter Jonsen and Juns Justasen, who in 1676, 3 years after settling it, bought the land from the Indians. Before 1684 Woola Erickson, Hans Petters, Andreas Homan and Israel Helm purchased tracts close to Repaupo Creek from the Swedish owners. Helm, one of the most prominent men of New Sweden, built his home on a 100-acre plot near the mouth of the creek and called it Helmstatt.

Scattered 100-acre plots do not constitute a community. But in the first days of Swedish and Finnish occupation of New Jersey, vast regions with relatively few settlers were known by general, all-inclusive names. Such was Repaupo, or Repaapo, as the Swedes originally called it, from the Indian word Repapack (*still water*), the name of the stream along which many of the farms were laid out. Rough enough to be called "the Wilderness," the country also had fine grazing and timber land which attracted settlers from across the river. Soon the district along Delaware River became known as Repaupo Meadows.

The Swedes and the Indians must have been on good terms, to judge from Peter Kalm's report of the early days when "the Indians lived with the Swedes." According to Kalm, some of the settlers laid a wager with a young Indian that he could not overtake a frog given a two-leap handi-

Port Elizabeth, where Swedes settled in the last half of the seventeenth century

PORT ELIZABETH

lica families, the Cobbs, the Kyns, the Petersons, the Moslanders and the Hopmans, all were represented among the earliest settlers.

The site of what is now Port Elizabeth was purchased by John Purple about 1720, and Swedes soon bought adjoining land. New immigrants by twos and threes paddled up the river and into its various tributaries, settling at great distances from one another. When Nicholas Collin came to preach here 50 years later, he "rode astray in the wilderness all afternoon" in his search for the community.

The colonists were dependent on the parishes of Raccoon and Penns Neck for their religious services. The Swedish pastors from these more important centers visited the area occasionally and preached at the centrally situated home of Goevan Kyn. This connection continued for about two years after formation of a separate parish in 1743. When Kyn, a widower, married Margaret Justis, a widow, in 1745, it was necessary to publish the banns in Raccoon and Penns Neck, as well as in the Maurice River settlement. Even though two acres of land had been bought from John Hoffman when the congregation was organized, the local church was not yet finished, so the wedding ceremony was held at the groom's home in the presence of "the entire Swedish congregation."

Because this was one of the pastorless periods in Swedish-New Jersey history, the church, when it was finally completed, was served by the Moravian brethren, peripatetic missionaries among both the Swedes and the Germans. Bryzelius, a Moravian who had been holding services at Raccoon and Penns Neck, preached the first sermon in the new church in 1745. Another Moravian, the Swedish Count Abraham Reinicke, performed the dedicatory service the following year. Swedish was still used by the preachers in 1748, as is shown by a record of a baptism which took place "at the close of the Swedish sermon."

When the Swedish Consistory once more began sending pastors to New Jersey, the Maurice River church replaced its Moravian preachers with Lutherans. Eric Unander, Johan Abraham Lidenius, Johan Wicksell and Nicholas

Collin were active in the area until about the time of the Revolution.

In 1771 John Bell bought what is now Port Elizabeth and sold it to Mrs. Elizabeth Clark Bodly, who laid out the town and supplied it with a name in 1785. In that year Congress named Port Elizabeth, then a glass manufacturing and shipbuilding center, as a port of entry.

Later, when the glass factory was moved to nearby Millville and the shipbuilding industry was brought closer to Delaware River, Port Elizabeth's business disappeared along with the old church on the river bank. Maurice River has covered both church and burial ground, and all of the tombstones and bones of the pioneers have been washed away—except for two markers, those of Hezekiah Lore and his wife, Elizabeth. These markers were removed to the Methodist Episcopal churchyard more than 50 years ago. The site of the old church and graveyard, now the yard for an unpretentious summer home, is on a wide bend of the river amidst a heavy growth of bayberry and blackberry bushes, oaks, Jersey pine and cedar trees.

XX
FRIESBURG CHURCH

BOTH Swedes and Germans settled the Cohansey district along the upper reaches of Alloway and Cohansey Creeks. Having the same religious creed, they cooperated to form the Lutheran congregation which, unlike the others formed in South Jersey, still retains its original faith. In the last decade of the seventeenth century, the Rev. Justus Falckner, a widely traveled German theological student, organized a mission which, in 1726, became the Emanuel Evangelical Lutheran Church, under the direction of the Rev. Peter Tranberg, Swedish pastor at Raccoon and Penns Neck.

In 1739, while Tranberg was still pastor, young Jacob Fries, a Hollander, donated land for a church. The community then became Friesburg. The congregation erected its first church building, a one-room log cabin, near the spot where the present church stands. Tranberg served the congregation as visiting pastor until he was transferred to Christina in 1741. He was followed by the Rev. Gabriel Näsman, the Wicacoa minister, whose irregular trips to New Jersey included visits to Friesburg as well as to Raccoon, Penns Neck and the Maurice River settlement. After a period during which pastors were supplied by the German Lutheran Synod, the Rev. Johan Abraham Lidenius officiated at Friesburg. From 1763-65 the Penns Neck and Raccoon minister, the Rev. Johan Wicksell, performed services. Wicksell, who could speak little English, was the last Swedish pastor to come to Friesburg.

In 1768 part of the narrow red brick church was built; the addition was built 100 years later. The simple building, with long straight lines rising symmetrically to the peaked roof, is practically surrounded by the old graveyard filled with stones inscribed in German. The name Fries, dating back to Jacob Fries and his many children, appears on many of the old gravestones. Swedish names are few.

Light-colored, well-kept farmhouses are spaced at intervals along the road. The church, standing alone, does not mark a community center any more than the widespread houses and broad, sown acres suggest a community.

Only surviving Lutheran Church in the New Sweden area of New Jersey, Friesburg

XXI

FORT ELFSBORG

FORT ELFSBORG now lies beneath the Delaware River. Only wild marshes, hardly providing a pathway, are opposite the place where in 1643 the fort was erected on an island, probably divided from New Jersey's mainland by these same swamps. The narrow strip of sand that borders the Delaware to the north drops entirely into the river in the Elfsborg area. Tangled growth and small, shaggy trees cover the tiny ditches and the dark, spongy muck, incapable of supporting a weight much greater than the bushes that hold it together. It is a dismal place.

Late in the nineteenth century, cannon balls, "one as large as a teacup, others smaller," were found here, but there is no evidence that they came from the old fort. Some investigators have recently found old wooden pilings which they claim to be parts of Elfsborg. This is highly questionable, for an old resident of the Delaware shore reported in 1874 that during his lifetime the river had eaten away 15 acres of land.

Governor Printz built the fort in 1643, "a little south of Mill Creek," at the narrowest part of the Delaware, strategically situated to command the stream and render valueless the Dutch Fort Nassau to the north. Printz had been instructed to build a fort by which "it should be possible to close up" the river. Actual construction of the earthwork began in March 1643, less than a month after Printz came to New Sweden. The stronghold was built "on the English plan with three angles close by the river," which probably means that it was in the shape of a semioctagon, with the rear open to the marsh.

A "beautiful portal" was constructed by the company's carpenter, and "eight 12 pound iron and brass guns and one mortar" were mounted. This was the best garrisoned fort on Delaware River, with 14 soldiers, 5 officers and

7 peasants and freemen. During the first year, however, nine of the garrison died. Lieutenant Sven Skute, New Sweden's second-in-command, was the officer in charge of the stronghold; Gregorius van Dyck (sergeant), Johan Mattsson (gunner) and Sven Andersson (drummer) were the other officers. Corporal Carl Hackensson was one of those who died during the first year. The Indians were not altogether friendly hereabouts, and Swedish settlers were occasionally killed on their way from Elfsborg to Christina. The natives once invaded the "island" on which the fort was being built, and burned part of the planks cut and sawed for a boat that was under construction.

In 1644 Printz reported, somewhat enigmatically and certainly sarcastically, that "Elfsborg . . . now (especially on the one side) is so secure that there is no need to fear any attack (if it is not entirely too severe) . . ." The fort was, at any rate, powerful enough to force foreign ships to strike colors, much to their chagrin and distress. Even before it was completed, on October 13, 1643, the Dutchman David De Vries halted his ship at command from the fortress and stood by until he was boarded and inspected. The arrogant Printz felt the power of his stronghold and used it imperiously. When William Aspinwall, commanding an English pinnace, drew abreast of Elfsborg in May 1644, Sven Skute fired a shot across his bow, "forcing [him] to fall lower and weigh anchor." Printz subsequently apologized but made Aspinwall pay for the powder and ball that stopped him. Andries Hudde, temporary commander at Fort Nassau, complained often of Printz's highhanded use of Fort Elfsborg, and in one of his reports to his superior claimed that by means of the fort Printz "held the river locked for himself." Adrien van der Donck, another Dutch official, complained even more bitterly that Printz "holds a high hand over each and all . . . who sail up into the South [Delaware] River, compelling them to strike their flags, without exception. He sends two men on board to inquire where they come from. Which is scarcely better than searching us, to which we expect it will come at last."

The marshes of New Jersey breed mosquitoes and gnats that early earned a reputation. The Swedes at Elfsborg nicknamed their fort "Myggenborg" or Mosquito Castle, and Israel Acrelius, the Swedish historian, mentions that the fort was "abandoned . . . and destroyed as it was almost impossible to live there on account of the gnats . . ." This legend acquired the distinction of fact among early historians, and was often mentioned when they discussed the fortress. Samuel Smith, who wrote in 1765, takes the credit from the gnats for the greater glory of the mosquito. ". . . The Musketoes were so numerous," he said, "the Swedes were unable to live here, and therefore removing, named the place Musketoeburgh.'"

In 1647 Printz reported that "Fort Elfsborg had been tolerably well fortified." The Swedes, however, withdrew in 1651 when the Dutch built Fort Casimir across the river and rendered Elfsborg impotent. The increasingly strong Dutch position and New Sweden's diminishing man power forced Printz to concentrate his forces at Fort New Gothenburg on the western shore. When Peter Stuyvesant, the Dutch Governor, sailed up the Delaware in 1655 to bring Governor Rising to heel, he stopped overnight at Fort Elfsborg, which "then lay in ruins." Here he reviewed his troops, who "shot and thundered all night."

Elfsborg during its lifetime was more than a fort; it was the first Swedish community on the Jersey shore and must have been self-supporting. Wherever the Swedes settled in the New World, they fished, hunted, trapped, and traded with the Indians, and, since Elfsborg was enough of a settlement to have its own pastor (Fluviander) during the first months of its existence, it is likely that many community enterprises were developed. Agriculture probably was one of them, for the tobacco raised in this section by English settlers was reported to be the best in the Colonies. And in Sweden there was a heavy demand for tobacco, which Printz did his utmost to fill.

As the fort fell to pieces, the river cut deeper and deeper into the mainland, covering the island on which Elfsborg stood. No attempt to mark the site was made except by early cartographers, who differed among themselves. The map makers agreed, however, on its approximate site, but so inexact were their charts that when the State recently erected a historical marker, it was placed relatively far inland, for only the general position of the stronghold could be determined.

CHRONOLOGY

1609   Henry Hudson, employed by Dutch East India Company, discovers South (Delaware) River.

1610   Samuel Argall names South River *Delaware* after English Governor de la Ware of Virginia.

c.1614   Manhattan settled by Dutch.

1623   Fort Nassau erected by Dutch near mouth of Timber Creek under Captain Cornelius Jacobson Mey.

1624   Gustavus Adolphus grants Willem Usselinx, Hollander, charter to form the South Company for world commerce.

1632   Usselinx commissioned general director of reorganized New South Company.
Gustavus Adolphus killed in battle at Lützen, Germany. Axel Oxenstierna, chancellor, becomes regent for six-year-old Queen Christina.

1634   Sir Edmund Plowden receives English grant including New Jersey section of Delaware River Valley.
Thomas Young makes unsuccessful attempt to found a settlement for Plowden at mouth of Pensauken Creek.

1635   Peter Minuit, former director-general of New Netherland, negotiates with Oxenstierna regarding Swedish settlement and trade in America.

1637   The New Sweden Company chartered for trade and settlement in the Delaware River Valley.
November 20. *Kalmar Nyckel* and *Fogel Grip* sail from Gothenburg, Sweden. Minuit commander of 26 colonists to found New Sweden.

1638   Swedes land during the middle of March two miles inland from Delaware River on Minquas Kill.
Fort Christina erected.
Minuit purchases territory from the Indians extending from Bomten's Point to the Schuylkill River on west bank of Delaware River.
Minuit lost at sea in West Indian hurricane.

1640   Peter Holländer Ridder arrives at Christina as second Governor of New Sweden. Second expedition brings the Rev. Reorous Torkillus, first Swedish Lutheran minister to serve in America. First church erected at Fort Christina.
Ridder purchases New Jersey territory from Cape May to Raccoon Creek. Increases Swedish lands on west bank of Delaware north to Sankikans, south to Cape Henlopen.

1641   Puritans from New Haven settle on Swedish territory at Varkens Kill. Swedes report inroads on their fur and tobacco trade.

154 SWEDES AND FINNS

1642   Ridder aids Dutch at New Netherland in destroying English settlement on the Schuylkill. Attempts to win over Varkens Kill colony to Sweden.

1643   February 15. New Sweden's "Golden Decade" begins with arrival of Johan Printz, third and greatest Governor of the colony.
Printz builds Fort Elfsborg near present city of Salem, controlling the Delaware Valley.
Varkens Kill settlement takes oath of allegiance to Sweden.
Construction of Printzhof, Fort Gothenburg and government buildings begun on Tinicum Island.
George Lamberton, former leader of Varkens Kill settlement, convicted of plot to incite Indian massacre of Swedes and Dutch in Delaware River Valley.

1644   Tinicum Island replaces Fort Christina as capital of New Sweden. Population of colony estimated at 121 people.
Klas Fleming, director of New Sweden Company, killed in Danish War.

1645   November 25. Tinicum Island buildings destroyed by fire. Printz rebuilds immediately.

1647   *Gyllene Haj* brings New Sweden first reinforcements in two years.
Fort New Korsholm built to control Schuylkill River against Dutch invasion.

1648   Population of colony estimated at 79 people.

1649   Printz buys region in New Jersey between Raccoon and Mantua Creeks.

1651   Peter Stuyvesant, director-general of New Netherland, decides to assert Dutch authority in Delaware River Valley.
June. Dutch build Fort Casimir, rendering Fort Elfsborg ineffective.
Printz dismantles Forts Elfsborg and New Korsholm and concentrates strength at Fort Gothenburg.

1652   Printz crushes rebellion on Tinicum Island.

1653   Printz names Johan Papegoja acting governor of colony and returns to Sweden via New Amsterdam.

1654   May 21. Johan Rising, successor to Printz, arrives in Delaware Valley.
Rising captures Fort Casimir and renames it **Fort Trefaldighet.**

1655   Stuyvesant captures New Sweden with a single casualty. Rising returns to Sweden. Nineteen Swedes swear allegiance to Holland.
Peter Lindeström, Swedish geographer, reports Swedes on Burlington Island.

CHRONOLOGY

1656   *Mercurius,* on twelfth expedition to New Sweden, arrives in Delaware Valley with 92 Finns and 13 Swedes aboard.

1661   Finns and Swedes believed to have settled at Finns Point.

1664   English conquer Delaware Valley.

1668   Ole Rasen, Cornelis Learson and Ole Jonson first Swedes to receive permit to buy land from the Indians in New Jersey. They purchase territory between Oldmans and Timber Creeks.
Peter Jegou and Fabrus Outhout represent Delaware settlements, including Swedish territory, at second session of Governor Philip Carteret's legislative assembly at Elizabethtown.

1673   Hans Hopman, Peter Jonsen and Juns Jastasen first Swedes to establish legal residence in New Jersey.

1675   Major John Fenwick and Quakers found Salem.

1676   Governor Edmund Andros upholds Swedish and Finnish land claims disputed by Fenwick.

1677   Swedish Mission established at Wicacoa (Philadelphia).

1682   Marked increase in migration of Pennsylvania and Delaware Swedes to Jersey shore.

1685   Peter Dalbo of Mantua first Swede to sit in legislative assembly.

1686   Gloucester County founded. Woola Dalbo named surveyor and road builder.

1690   Justus Falckner organizes Cohansey Mission.

1693   List of Swedish settlers in region formerly known as New Sweden names 139 families with 939 individuals.

1697   Eric Mullica at Lower Bank.

1699   Old Swedes (Christina) Church completed at Christina. Jersey Swedes provide funds, labor and material upon promise of similar aid later when a Jersey church was to be built.

1700   Gloria Dei (Wicacoa) Church completed.

1701   Lars Tollstadius arrives at Wicacoa.
Swedish school in New Jersey founded at Raccoon by Hans Stalt.
Tollstadius agitates for an independent church in New Jersey.

1702   Kings Highway reaches Swedish community at Raccoon Creek.

1703   Raccoon Parish founded by Tollstadius.

1706   Tollstadius drowned in Delaware River. The Rev. Jonas Aurén pastor at Raccoon.
Carl Brunjen founds first permanent Swedish school in New Jersey at Raccoon.

1713   The Rev. Abraham Lidenius named pastor of Raccoon Church, and begins keeping records of parish.

SWEDES AND FINNS

1714   Bishop Jesper Svedberg, of Skara, authorizes founding of St. George Church at Penns Neck (Churchtown).

1715   Swedish school established at Repaupo.

1717   March 31. St. George Church dedicated by Provost Andreas Sandel. Lidenius named pastor in addition to duties at Raccoon.

1720   Raccoon and St. George parishes purchase glebe or parsonage farm.

1724-26   Swedish churches pastorless.

1726   The Rev. Peter Tranberg and the Rev. Andrew Windrufwa serve in Raccoon and Penns Neck churches respectively.
Evangelical Lutheran Church organized from Cohansey Mission.

1728   Windrufwa dies in pleurisy epidemic. Raccoon and Penns Neck parishes reunited by Tranberg.

1741   Tranberg transferred to Christina parish. Moravian missionaries serve pastorless Swedish communities.

1742   Penns Neck congregation decides to have services in English and in "the manner of the Church of England."

1743   Maurice River Church organized by Swedes near present site of Port Elizabeth.

1745   Gloucester County Court restrains Moravians from preaching in English and Swedish churches.
Count Abraham Reinicke, Swedish-born Moravian, dedicates Maurice River church.

1748   The Rev. Johan Sandin arrives as pastor of Raccoon and Penns Neck churches and Dean of Swedish Evangelical Lutheran Churches in America. Raccoon becomes seat of Swedish ecclesiastical authority in America.
Peter Kalm, Finnish-Swedish naturalist and theology student, preaches at Raccoon and Penns Neck.

1749   The Rev. Eric Unander appointed rector of Raccoon and Penns Neck churches.

1750   The Rev. Israel Acrelius becomes Dean of Swedish churches in America and rector of Christina parish. New campaign to revive declining use of Swedish in churches begun.

1756   The Rev. Johan Abraham Lidenius becomes rector of Raccoon and Penns Neck churches.

1762   The Rev. Johan Wicksell chosen pastor of Raccoon and Penns Neck.

1763   Raccoon renamed Swedesboro.

1765   King George III grants English charter to Raccoon and Penns Neck parishes.

1768   Friesburg congregation erects brick building.

CHRONOLOGY

1770	The Rev. Nicholas Collin, last of Swedish ministers, serves as assistant to Wicksell at Raccoon and Penns Neck.
1773	Collin becomes rector of Raccoon and Penns Neck parishes.
1775	Swedes generally support Americans in the Revolutionary War.
1778	Swedish schoolhouse near Raccoon Church burned by British. Collin begins drive for new church building at Swedesboro.
1784	Swedish Evangelical Lutheran Church at Swedesboro dedicated.
1786	Swedish churches at Swedesboro (Raccoon Parish) and Penns Neck (St. George Parish) transferred to Episcopal Church of America.
1800	Swedes help found towns of Dorchester and Leesburg.
c.1825	Many Swedes move east into Cumberland and Cape May Counties.
1831	Collin dies at Philadelphia.
c.1850	Scandinavian immigration to United States begins.
1857	Many Swedes settle at Barnegat.
1874	*History of New Sweden,* by the Rev. Israel Acrelius, first published in English translation. Swedes prominent in founding towns of Franklinville and Malaga.
1889	First Swedish Lutheran Church founded in northern New Jersey at Dover.
1898	Upsala Institute moves from Brooklyn, N. Y., to Kenilworth, N. J.
1909	Swedish Colonial Society founded at Philadelphia.
1911	*The Swedish Settlements on the Delaware,* by Dr. Amandus Johnson, published.
1924	Upsala College moves to East Orange.
1930	Swedish and Swedish-American population of New Jersey totals 29,849; Finns and Finnish-Americans total 4,494
1938	Tercentenary Celebration of landing of the Swedes and Finns in Delaware River Valley.

BIBLIOGRAPHY

Archives of the State of New Jersey. Vols. IX, XXI and XXIII.

Barber, John W., and Howe, Henry. *Historical Collections of the State of New Jersey.* 512 p. il. S. Tuttle, New York, 1844.

Benson, Adolph B. trans. *Peter Kalm's Travels in North America.* 2 v. 797 p. il. Wilson-Erickson, Inc., New York, 1937.

Bowen, F. W. *History of Port Elizabeth, Cumberland County.* 102 p. il. Republished in 1936, Millville Publishing Company, Millville, N. J.

Brandt, Francis Burke. *The Majestic Delaware, the Nation's Foremost Historic River.* 182 p. il. Brandt and Gummere Company, Philadelphia.

Burr, Horace. trans. *Records of Old Swedes' Church, Wilmington, Delaware, 1697-1778.* 281 p. Historical Society of Delaware, Wilmington, 1890.

Clay, Rev. Jehu C. *Annals of the Swedes on the Delaware.* 179 p. 2nd ed. Published by the author, Philadelphia, 1858.

Clement, John. *Early Settlers of Newton Township.* 423 p. Sinnickson-Chew, Camden, 1877.

Cushing, Thomas and Sheppard, Charles E. *History of the Counties of Gloucester, Cumberland and Salem, New Jersey.* 728 p. il. Evarts and Peck, Philadelphia, 1883.

Elmer, Lucius Q. C. *Early History of Cumberland County,* 139 p. George F. Nixon, Bridgeton, 1869.

Extracts from the Records of Wicacoa (Gloria Dei) Church, 1750-1800. The Pennsylvania Magazine of History and Biography, V. 2. Historical Society of Pennsylvania, Philadelphia, 1879.

Federal Writers' Project of Delaware. *New Castle on the Delaware.* 138 p. il. Historical Society of Delaware, Wilmington, 1936.

Federal Writers' Project of New Jersey. trans. *Records of the Swedish Evangelical Lutheran Church, Swedesboro.* MS., 1937-38.

Ferris, Benjamin. *History of the Original Settlements on the Delaware and a History of Delaware.* 312 p. Wilson and Heald, Wilmington, 1846.

Janson, Florence E. *The Background of Swedish Immigration, 1840-1930.* 517 p. University of Chicago Press, Chicago, 1931.

BIBLIOGRAPHY

Johnson, Amandus. trans. and ed. *The Journal and Biography of Nicholas Collin.* 353 p. il. New Jersey Society of Pennsylvania, Philadelphia, 1937.

────── trans. *Geographica Americae With an Account of the Delaware Indians Based on Notes Made by Peter Lindeström.* 418 p. il. and maps. Swedish Colonial Society, Philadelphia, 1925.

────── trans. *Report about the Mines in the United States of America,* by Samuel Gustaf Hermelin, 1783. 82 p. The John Morton Museum, Philadelphia, 1931.

────── *The Swedes on the Delaware, 1638-1664.* 377 p. il. International Printing Company, Philadelphia, 1927.

────── *Swedish Settlements on the Delaware, 1638-1664.* 2 v. 763 p. il. New Era Publishing Company, Lancaster, 1911.

Johnson, Robert Gibbon. *An Historical Account of the Settlement of Salem in West Jersey by John Fenwick, Esquire.* 173 p. Orin G. Rogers, Philadelphia, 1839.

Leaming, Aaron, and Spicer, Jacob. *Grants and Concessions of New Jersey.* 753 p. 2nd ed. Honeyman and Company, Somerville, 1881.

Lee, Francis Bazley. *New Jersey as a Colony and as a State.* 4 v. il. Publishing Society of New Jersey, New York, 1903.

Louhi, E. A. *The Delaware Finns.* 331 p. Humanity Press, New York, 1925.

Mickle, Isaac. *Reminiscences of Old Gloucester: or Incidents in the History of Gloucester, Atlantic and Camden, New Jersey.* 98 p. il. Townsend Wood, Philadelphia, 1845.

Myers, Albert Cook. trans. and ed. *Narratives of Pennsylvania, West New Jersey and Delaware.* 459 p. Charles Scribner's Sons, New York, 1912.

Paxson, Henry D. *Swedes of North America.* 248 p. il. Swedish Colonial Society, Philadelphia, 1926.

────── *Where Pennsylvania History Began.* 241 p. il. Swedish Colonial Society, Philadelphia, 1926.

Records of the Court at New Castle 1676-1681. Colonial Society of Pennsylvania, Lancaster, 1904.

Record of the Court at Upland, in Pennsylvania, 1676-1681. Historical Society of Pennsylvania, Philadelphia, 1860.

Reynolds, William M. trans. *History of New Sweden, or the Settlements on the River Delaware,* by Israel Acrelius, 1759. 468 p. Historical Society of Pennsylvania, Philadelphia, 1874.

Shourds, Thomas. *History and Genealogy of Fenwick's Colony.* 553 p. il. George F. Nixon, Bridgeton, 1876.

Sickler, Joseph S. *History of Salem County.* 374 p. Sunbeam Publishing Company, Salem, 1937.

Stewart, Frank H. *Notes on Old Gloucester County.* 3 v. Historical Society of Gloucester County (N. J.), Woodbury, 1935.

Stomberg, Andrew A. *History of Sweden.* 797 p. il. Macmillan Company, New York, 1931.

Taylor, Benjamin. *Annals of the Classis of Bergen, of the Reformed Dutch Church, and of the Churches Under its Care. Including the Civil History of the Ancient Township of Bergen.* Board of Publication of the Reformed Protestant Dutch Church, New York, 1857.

Ward, Christopher. *The Dutch and Swedes on the Delaware.* 378 p. University of Pennsylvania Press, Philadelphia, 1930.

Wuorinen, John H. *The Finns in Delaware, 1638-1655.* Columbia University Press, New York, 1938.

INDEX

Åbo (Turku), 84
Absequam Beach, 68
Acrelius, the Rev. Israel, 16, 84, 85, 87, 88, 89, 93, 94, 96, 98, 105, 122, 123, 135, 151
Agriculture, 30, 39, 45, 58, 66, 72, 91, 151
All Hail to Thee, O Blessed Morn, 109
Alloways Creek, 68, 83, 147
Amsterdam, 7, 22, 54
Anderson, Andreas (Homan), 64, 91, 140
Anderson, Andrew, 67
Anderson, Juste, 67
Anderson, Matthew and Lasse, 141
Andersson, Sven, 150
Andros, Governor Edmund, 63
Angelsea, 106, 107
Argall, Capt. Samuel, 14
Arlington, 108, 111
Asbury, 142
Aspinwall, William, 150
Atlantic City, 68, 107
Atlantic County, 69, 106, 107
Aurén, the Rev. Jonas, 76, 77, 78, 118, 119, 132

Baltic Lands, 6
Baltic Sea, 42
Baltimore, Lord, 15
Barbadoes Islands, 54
Barnegat, 104
Beard, Charles A., 8
Bell, John, 146
Bergen County, 107
Berkeley, Governor William, 19
Berkeley, Lord John, 63
Big Timber Creek, 61, 65, 66, 87
Björk, the Rev. Eric, 74, 75, 76, 78, 83, 116, 117, 118, 130, 131, 132
Bjuråkers Handskrift, 109
Blommaert, Samuel, 6, 7, 8, 9, 10, 11, 17, 18, 28, 30
Bodly, Elizabeth Clark, 146
Bomten's Point, 19, 25
Brazil, 3
Bromfield, Will., 62
Brunjen, Carl, 78, 118
Bryzelius, Paul Daniel, 82, 83, 84, 122, 145
Burlington County, 106, 108
Burlington Island, 60, 62

Cabot, John, 14, 15
Calvert, Governor Leonard, 29
Camden County, 107
Campanius, John (Holm.), 73, 79
Cape Henlopen, 25, 33
Cape Lookout, 17
Cape May, 15, 25, 69, 115
Cape May County, 102, 106, 107
Carribbean Sea, 18, 21
Carteret, Governor Philip, 61, 62, 63, 140
Cattle raising, 24, 30, 72, 91
Charles I, King of England, 16, 17, 26
Charles IX, King of Sweden, 3
Chesapeake Bay, 22
Childs, Marquis W., 114
Christina Church, 73, 74, 77, 81, 116, 117, 130, 131, 132, 133, 134, 147
Christina Creek (*see* Minquas Kill)
Christina, Queen of Sweden, 5, 19, 51
Church Landing Road, 136
Cinnaminson (Senamensing), 64, 65, 77
Clay, the Rev. Jehu C., 100, 103
Clothing, Swedish, 89
Cock, Laurentz, 80
Cohansey River, 68, 83, 147
Collin, the Rev. Nicholas, 85, 88, 90, 91, 94, 97, 98, 99, 100, 103, 124, 125, 126, 135, 136, 142, 145, 146
Colman, Lacy (Lasse), 62, 67
Colonial claims, 16, 20, 25, 26
Commercial College of Sweden, 51
Consistory of Uppsala, 71, 78, 81, 82, 84, 96, 99, 110, 119, 121, 123, 124, 132, 145
Cooperatives, 113, 114
Copper trade, 6, 7
Corvon, Paul, 62
Cumberland County, 61, 102, 107

Dalbo, Anders, 137, 138
Dalbo family, 64, 65, 67, 70, 77, 128
Dalbo, Peter, 64, 65, 67, 91
Dalbo, Woola, 64, 66, 141
Dalbo's Landing, 106
Dalbow, William, 98
Danish War, 42, 43
Delaware, 13, 16, 17, 63

SWEDES AND FINNS

Delaware Bay, 14, 18, 53, 102
Delaware River, 1, 3, 7, 8, 10, 14, 16, 18, 24, 25, 29, 30, 31, 36, 43, 47, 50, 52, 53, 54, 57, 58, 65, 67, 68, 70, 71, 105, 115, 129, 130, 134, 139, 140, 144, 146, 149, 151
Delaware Valley, 7, 13, 14, 22, 25, 45, 46, 76, 103
De la Warr, Lord, 14
Denmark, 2, 3, 42
De Vries, David, 34, 150
Didricsson, Manne, 119
Dircks, Oele, 62
Dorchester, 102
Dover, 108, 111
Dutch East India Company, 14
Dutch West India Company, 4 ,7, 8, 14, 15, 19, 22, 23, 26, 47, 53, 54

East Indies, 7
East Orange, 108, 111, 112
Elbe River, 19
Eliot, John, 73
Elk River, 118
Elsinborough Township, 106
England and English, 1, 3, 15, 16, 17, 24, 25, 26, 34, 38, 57, 59, 61, 82, 87, 88, 93, 100
English language, growth of, 70, 71, 76, 79, 82, 85, 86, 87, 97, 124
Epidemics, 92
Episcopal Church in America, 99, 136
Erickson, Peter, 65
Erickson, Woola, 140
Ericson, Lief, 2
Erixson, John, 67
Essex County, 108
Eurinson, Hendrick, 67

Falckner, Justus, 83, 147
Fama, the, 30, 31, 33, 38, 42, 64
Fenwick, Maj. John, 62, 63, 67, 130
Finland, 3
Finland, Gulf of, 4
Finns Point, 60, 63, 69, 77, 129, 130, 135
Finns Town, 60
Fleming, Klas, 10, 23, 27, 42
Florida, 16
Fluviander, the Rev. Israel, 73, 151
Flying Stag, the, 21
Fogel Grip, the, 11, 12, 18, 19, 20, 23
Foods, 90
Fort Beversreede, 47, 48
Fort Casimir (later Fort Trefaldighet), 49, 52, 53, 54, 55, 56, 151

Fort Christina, 18, 20, 22, 23, 24, 26, 27, 28, 30, 34, 37, 38, 39, 43, 49, 52, 53, 55, 56, 59, 60, 79, 89
Fort Elfsborg, 33, 34, 37, 38, 39, 41, 47, 48, 49, 52, 54, 73, 89, 149-152
Fort Nassau, 3, 14, 15, 19, 20, 25, 32, 33, 44, 47, 49, 149, 150
Fort New Gothenburg, 35, 38, 49, 51, 55, 56, 60, 151
Fort New Korsholm, 44, 49, 53
France, 1, 3, 6, 16, 24
Franklin, Benjamin, 103
Franklinville, 105
Freeman, Peter, 62
Frenne, Gabriel, 122
Friesburg Church, 68, 83, 86, 147-148
General Assembly, 62, 65, 66
Germany, 1, 5, 6, 24, 42
Glebe, the (Parsonage Farm), 78, 121, 137-139
Gloria Dei Church (*see* Wicacoa)
Gloucester, 14, 68
Gloucester County, 61, 64, 65, 66, 67, 98, 105, 106, 107
Godyn, Samuel, 14
Gold Coast, 9
Gothenburg, 2, 3, 4, 5, 10, 11, 12, 23, 34, 42, 71
Great Egg Harbor, 68
Guinea, 6, 8
Gustafson, Nils, 93
Gustavsson, Gustav, 122
Gustavus Adolphus, King of Sweden, 1, 2, 3, 4, 5, 6, 70
Gyllene Haj, the, 43, 44, 53, 54

Hackensonn, Corp. Carl, 150
Half Moon, the, 14
Halton, Peter, 67
Hamburg, 9
Hance, John, 65
Helm, Capt. Israel, 63, 64, 66, 68, 120, 122, 140
Helm, Ingeborg, 68
Helm's Cove, 67, 69, 106
Helmstatt, 64, 140
Hendrickson, David, 98
Hendricson, Jacob, 67
Hermelin, Samuel Gustaf, 102
Hesselius, the Rev. Samuel, 133, 134
Heuling, John, 98
Hindricsson, Hindric, 122
Hockhammen and Company, Henry, 79
Hoffman, Joannes, 122
Hoffman, John, 145
Hog marking, 91

INDEX

Holland, 1, 3, 4, 6, 8, 10, 12, 16, 57, 59
Holm, Thomas Campanius, 85, 103
Homan (*see* Anderson, Andreas)
Hopman, Hans, 61, 62, 140
Hopman, John, 91
Hudde, Andries, 150
Hudson County, 108
Hudson, Henry, 14
Hudson River, 13, 14, 53
Hugg, John, 117
Huygen, Hendrick, 11, 20, 22, 23, 25, 28, 32, 43, 44, 50

Immigration, Scandinavian, 104
  German, 68, 70, 71
India, 3
Indian trade, 20, 22, 23, 25, 26, 28, 37, 42, 50
Indians, 7, 15, 19, 25, 30, 32, 35, 39, 40, 48, 53, 54, 57, 115, 150, 151
Industries, 24, 39, 45, 102
Intermarriage, 72, 101
International Order of Good Templars, 111

Jacobson, John, 67
Jacques (or James) Island, 33, 35
Jamestown, 3, 19, 36
Jaquet, Jean, 133
Jersey City, 108, 109, 111
Johnson, Dr. Amandus, 7, 11, 16, 17, 25, 35, 41, 52, 91, 105
Jonsen, Peter, 61, 140
Jonson, Ole, 61, 140
Julafton, 109, 110
Julotta, 109, 110
Justasen, Juns, 61, 62, 140
Justasen, Måns, 62
Justis, Margaret, 145

Kalm, Peter, 58, 84, 85, 88, 89, 90, 91, 92, 102, 123, 134, 135, 140, 141
Kalmar Nyckel, the, 10, 12, 18, 20, 23, 24, 42
Keen, John, 139
Keen, Måns, 92
Kenilworth, 112
Kent, the, 63
Kieft, Director-General, 20, 22, 23, 26, 36, 37, 41
King, Frederick, 65
Kings Highway, 65, 66, 69, 98, 117, 124, 127, 128, 137, 141
Kling, Måns, 20, 22, 23, 25, 27, 31, 44, 45
Kyn, Goevan, 145

Laikian, Michael, 137
Lamberton, George, 36, 37, 38
Land acquisitions, 19, 25, 45
Land use, 58, 92
Laury, William, 11
Lawrence, Markus (Hallings), 65
Learson, Cornelis, 61, 140
Leesburg, 102
Lidenius, the Rev. Abraham, 77, 78, 81, 82, 96, 119, 120, 123, 133, 134, 137, 138
Lidenius, the Rev. Johan Abraham, 86, 123, 145, 147
Lindeström, Peter, 58, 60
Little Mantoes (Mantua), 65
Lock, Lars, 73, 122
Log cabins, Swedish, 89
Long Island, 15
Lore, Hezekiah and Elizabeth, 146
Lower Penns Neck, 60
Lützen, Battle of, 5

Malander, Olaf, 121, 134, 138
Manhattan, 20, 23, 27, 35, 45
Mantua Creek, 64, 67, 75, 91
Marriage customs, 93, 94
Marthin, Sven, 107
Maryland, 32, 59
Mattsson, Johann, 150
Maurice River, 77, 102, 144, 145, 146, 147
Maurice River Church (Port Elizabeth Church), 83, 86, 97, 145
Maurice River Valley, 61, 68, 70
Mazarin, Cardinal, 6
Mekekanchken Island, 45
Mercurius, the, 60
Mexico, 3, 11
Mey, Capt. Cornelius Jacobsen, 14
Minquas Kill (Christina Creek), 18, 19, 20, 23, 30, 67
Minuit, Peter, 7, 8, 9, 10, 11, 17, 18, 19, 20, 22, 23, 24, 25, 26, 30, 39, 41, 57
Mölndal, 43, 49
Montclair, 108, 111
Moravians, 74, 82, 83, 84, 122, 123, 134, 145
Mullica, 69
Mullica, Eric Sr., 68, 69, 102, 106
Mullica Hill, 68, 69
Mullica River, 69

Names, Anglicization of, 72, 106
Näsman, the Rev. Gabriel, 122, 134, 147

SWEDES AND FINNS

Neilson, Anthony, 65, 66, 142
Nelson, William, 60
New Albion, 15
New Amsterdam, 16, 50, 55
Newark, 108, 111
New Castle, 61, 63
New England, 25, 53
New Netherland, 7, 8, 16, 40, 41, 44, 47, 48, 53, 55, 56
New Stockholm, 20, 62, 63, 106
New Sweden Crossroads, 106
Norrköping, 5
North Plainfield, 111
North Sea, 12
Nortonville, 106
Norway, 2
Nothnagle House, 65, 142

Oldmans Creek, 61, 65, 66, 69, 129
Orn, the, 51, 52
Oxenstierna, Axel, 2, 3, 4, 5, 6, 7, 8, 9, 17, 21, 23, 27, 31, 42, 49
Oxenstierna, Count Johan, 16
Oxenstierna, Eric, 51

Papegoja, Johan, 44, 50, 51, 53, 60
Paradise Point, 18
Passaic County, 108
Penn, William, 63, 64
Penns Neck, 64, 67, 69, 70, 77, 78, 79, 81, 86, 96, 97, 98, 99, 121, 129-136, 137, 139, 145, 147
Penns Neck Bridge, 67
Penns Neck Township, 67
Pennsville, 61
Pennsylvania, 13, 66, 68, 76
Pensauken Creek, 15, 62, 65, 68, 77, 79
Peru, 3, 11
Peter the Great, 2
Peterson, Lucas, 67
Petri, Olavus, 109
Petters, Hans, 140
Philadelphia, 33, 68, 107, 126, 128, 129, 134
Philip II, King of Spain, 5
Pierson, John, 127
Pilesgrove, 137
Plowden, Lord Edmund, 15, 26, 34, 36
Plymouth, 3, 11
Poland, 2, 3
Port Elizabeth, 144-146
Port Norris, 102
Portugal, 3, 32
Powelson, Powell, 67

Printz, Governor Johan, 29, 30, 31, 32, 33, 34, 35, 36, 37, 38, 39, 40, 41, 42, 43, 44, 45, 46, 47, 48, 50, 51, 52, 53, 57, 59, 64, 73, 85, 114, 149, 150, 151
Purple, John, 145

Quakers, 63, 70, 79

Raccoon (Swedesboro), 62, 64, 65, 69, 70, 71, 76, 77, 78, 79, 81, 84, 86, 91, 92, 93, 94, 96, 101, 113-128, 137, 139, 141, 142, 145, 147
Raccoon Church, 76, 77, 78, 81, 82, 83, 84, 86, 96, 98, 99, 110, 132
Raccoon Creek (New Stockholm River), 25, 60, 62, 63, 67, 75, 76, 115, 117, 124, 127
Rambo family, the, 64, 67, 70, 77, 98, 103, 105
Rambo, John, 64, 65
Rambo, Peter, 63, 65
Rasen, Ole, 61, 140
Reading (Pa.), 96
Reeve, Peter, 102
Reinicke, Count Abraham, 123, 145
Repaupo, 64, 65, 71, 77, 79, 85, 88, 103, 106, 140-143
Revolutionary War, 98, 124, 135, 142
Ridder, Governor Peter Holländer, 23, 24, 25, 26, 27, 28, 29, 30, 31, 33, 36, 37, 40, 41, 57, 115
Rising, Governor Johan, 16, 17, 51, 52, 53, 54, 55, 56, 57, 59, 151
Roanoke (N. C.), 17
Roseland, 111
Rotterdam, 21
Rudman, the Rev. Andrew, 75, 76, 83
Runnels, Eric, 122
Russia, 2, 3
Rutabagas, 90, 91

St. Christopher, 20
St. George Church (Penns Neck), 77, 78, 81, 82, 83, 84, 85, 96, 98, 99, 133, 136
St. John Episcopal Church, 136
Salem, 80, 87, 105, 126, 136
Salem County, 62, 68, 77, 98, 106, 107
Salem Creek, 26, 60, 62, 67, 79, 129
Salvation Army, 111
Sandel, the Rev. Andreas, 75, 76, 78, 83, 117
Sandin, the Rev. Johan, 84, 123, 134, 138
Sankikans (Trenton Falls), 33, 45
Schools, Swedish, 74, 78, 79, 116

INDEX

Quaker, 72
Schuylkill River, 14, 15, 19, 25, 26, 37, 38, 44, 47, 48
"Semla bullar," 110
Sinnickson, Capt. Andrew, 98
Skute, Lieut. Sven, 54, 150
Smith, Capt. John, 29
South River (Delaware), 14, 150
Spain, 3, 11, 16
Spiring, Peter, 8, 9, 10, 21, 27, 30, 43
Stålt, Hans, 74, 116, 117, 131
States-General (the Netherlands), 4
Steelman Bay, 69
Steelman, James, 68, 69, 102, 106
Steelman Thoroughfare, 69
Steelman's Landing, 69
Steelmantown, 69
Steelmanville, 69
Stewart, Frank H., 91
Stillman, Hans, 122
Stockholm, 1, 10, 22, 71
Stomberg, Dr. Andrew, 6
Stumpff, Joachim, 9
Stuyvesant, Governor Peter, 29, 47, 48, 49, 53, 54, 55, 56, 59, 151
Svedberg, Bishop Jesper, 77
Swan, the, 30, 31, 33, 45, 46
Swanendael, 14
Swanson, Walla, 65
Swedesboro (Raccoon), 62, 66, 96, 97, 98, 106, 113-128
Swedish Baptist Church, 111
Swedish Cultural Society, 112
Swedish Evangelical Mission Covenant, 111
Swedish Folk Festival Society, 111
Swedish Literary Society De Nio, 112
Swedish Methodist Church, 111
Swedes Run, 106

Tacony, 68
Tax list, Gloucester County, 1687, 66
Terra Nova (Newfoundland), 16
Texel, 12
Thirty Years' War, 6, 7, 24
Thomas, Gabriel, 68
Thompson's Point, 64
Tinicum Island, 35, 42, 43, 49, 53, 73, 89
Tobacco, 19, 39, 93
Tollstadius, Lars, 74, 75, 76, 82, 94, 98, 103, 111, 114, 117, 118, 131, 132
Torkillus, the Rev. Reorus, 23
Toy, Elias, 65

Toy, Susannah, 68
Trading Companies, 2
  South Company, the, 4, 5
  New South Company, the, 5
  New Sweden Company, the, 9, 10, 15, 17, 23, 28, 35, 48, 50, 51, 60, 81
Tranberg, the Rev. Peter, 81, 84, 120, 121, 134, 147
Trinity Episcopal Church (formerly Raccoon Church), 99, 117, 126, 127, 128
Trumpeter's Creek, 65
Turner, Capt. Nathaniel, 26

Ulrica, Queen of Sweden, 120
Unander, the Rev. Eric, 84, 86, 96, 123, 134, 139, 145
Union County, 108
United New Netherland Company, 14
Upland, 38, 40, 64
Upper Penns Neck, 98
Uppsala, 112, 117
Upsala College, 112, 113
Usselinx, Willem, 4, 5, 7, 8, 9, 15, 17
Utrecht, 26

Varkens Kill (*see* Salem Creek)
Varkens Kill, settlement at, 26, 32, 33, 34, 36, 38
Vasa Order of America, 107, 112
Vass, Sven, 43
Vikings, 2, 14
Viking Lodge, 112
Vineland, 2
Virginia, 3, 8, 14, 15, 19, 32, 35, 38, 59
van der Donck, Adrien, 150
van Dyck, Gregorius, 150
Vanneman, Helmes, 103
Vasa, House of, 2, 71

Wade, the Rev. John, 136
Ward, Christopher, 35
West Indies, 7
White Gift Sunday, 110
Wicacoa Church (Gloria Dei), 65, 73, 74, 81, 103, 116, 117, 121, 147
Wicksell, the Rev. Johan, 96, 97, 98, 123, 124, 139, 145, 147
Wilmington (Del.), 20, 83
Windrufwa, the Rev. Andrew, 134
Winthrop, Governor John, 29, 38
Woodbury Creek, 65

Young, Thomas, 15

Zinzendorf, Count von, 122

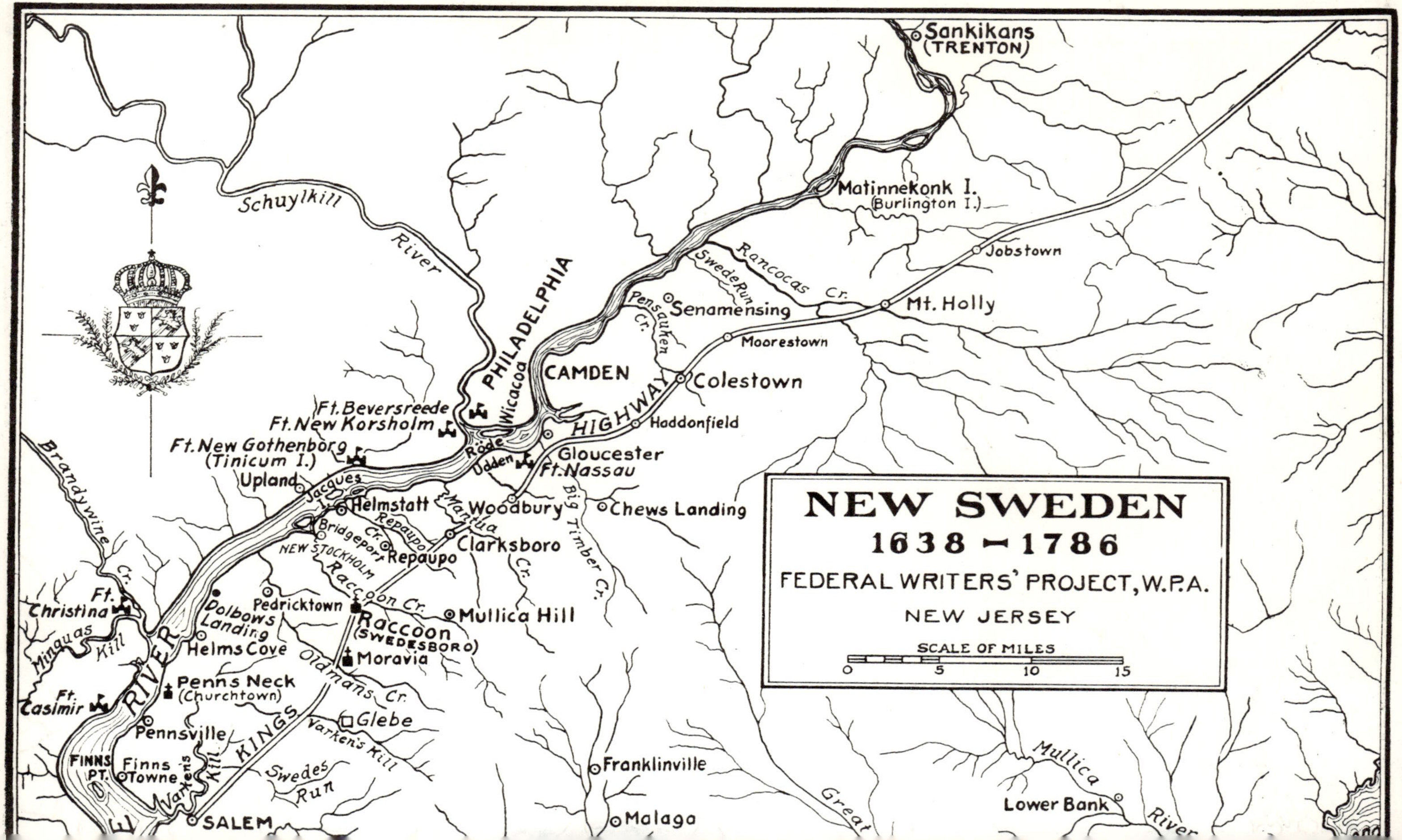
NEW SWEDEN
1638 – 1786
FEDERAL WRITERS' PROJECT, W.P.A.
NEW JERSEY
SCALE OF MILES
0
5
10
15
Sankikans
(TRENTON)
Matinnekonk I.
(Burlington I.)
Jobstown
Mt. Holly
Rancocas Cr.
Swede Run
Senamensing
Moorestown
Colestown
Pensauken Cr.
CAMDEN
PHILADELPHIA
Wicacoa
HIGHWAY
Haddonfield
Gloucester
Ft. Nassau
Schuylkill River
Ft. Beversreede
Ft. New Korsholm
Ft. New Gothenborg
(Tinicum I.)
Röde
Udden
Upland
Jacques I.
Helmstatt
Woodbury
Chews Landing
Big Timber Cr.
Mantua Cr.
Repaupo Cr.
Bridgeport
NEW STOCKHOLM
Repaupo
Clarksboro
Raccoon Cr.
Pedricktown
Mullica Hill
Raccoon
(SWEDESBORO)
Moravia
Dolbows Landing
Helms Cove
Oldmans Cr.
Brandywine Cr.
Ft. Christina
Minquas Kill
Ft. Casimir
RIVER
Penns Neck
(Churchtown)
Glebe
KINGS
Varken's Kill
Pennsville
FINNS PT.
Finns Towne
Swedes Run
SALEM
Franklinville
Malaga
Great
Mullica River
Lower Bank